I0790429

Also by James Michael Matthew

Prophecy before Vision

- ➢ Author Shout 2023 Reader Ready Award
- ➢ American Writing Awards Winner 2022
- ➢ New England Book Festival Award 2022
- ➢ New York Book Festival honorable mention 2022
- ➢ Full page feature & social media on Second Quarter 2023 issue of Bookmad

Reject Self-Serving Power

- ➢ The BREW Book Excellence Award 2023
- ➢ Indies Today Award 2022
- ➢ London Book Festival Award 2023

Building the Climate Change Bridge

- ➢ LA Times Festival of Books 2023

Defeating the New Axis Powers

THE TWO $20 TRILLION OPPORTUNITIES

PART 3 OF BUILDING
THE CLIMATE CHANGE BRIDGE SERIES

Planning The Selfless Economy Fixing Our Financial Mess

JAMES MICHAEL MATTHEW

Archway Publishing books may be ordered through booksellers or by contacting:

Archway Publishing
1663 Liberty Drive
Bloomington, IN 47403
www.archwaypublishing.com
844-669-3957

ISBN: 978-1-6657-4256-6 (sc)
ISBN: 978-1-6657-4254-2 (hc)
ISBN: 978-1-6657-4255-9 (e)

Library of Congress Control Number: 2023907370

Print information available on the last page.

Archway Publishing rev. date: 05/04/2023

This book is dedicated to all the people of the world who are wondering how we can pay for climate change, save the planet for future generations, pay the world's debts, and fix our financial mess.

CONTENTS

ACKNOWLEDGMENTS

I want to acknowledge all the companies and universities in our
nation and around the world that are pioneering self-assembly.
As will be discussed in chapter 19 and others in this book, the
work they have begun should be an inspiration to all of us as
we begin to understand the possibilities for the future.

INTRODUCTION

The Two $20 Trillion Opportunities is the third and final book in a three-part series dedicated to providing new solutions for solving the critical problems brought on by global warming, climate change, rising ocean coastlines, biodiversity loss, desertification, ocean pollution, and fresh water depletion. This book (my fifth) focuses on paying for climate change and preparing for the end of natural resources and lays out a map to begin building the climate change bridge. My third book, *Building the Climate Change Bridge,* built the platform for how we can transition from fossil fuels to being a green-energy-based society—a bridge to get us there from here. My fourth book, *Defeating the New Axis Powers,* focused on the geopolitical issues related to climate change.

This book also sets forth a plan to create the selfless economy, which we first began studying together in my second book, *Reject Self-Serving Power.* I include financial plans to pay for both building the climate change bridge and building the selfless economy.

I have been fortunate to have discussions with concerned citizens at my book signings, who have confirmed to me that I am on the right track. One conversation that sums up what I constantly heard was my discussion with a lady from Indiana who had three sons aged eighteen to late twenties. They were all upper-middle class and obviously already successful in life. But they were all concerned about their sons' futures, the future of our country, and the future of the planet.

It is no secret that most in the nation share the same concerns and anxieties. There is growing doubt about any responsible leadership or strategies for moving forward as a society. This book was written to provide the nation with a plan for our future.

I believe there are two $20 trillion opportunities for the future that are waiting for our nation to embrace. The first is pursuing the goal of 5 percent usable fresh water for climate change. The second is building a selfless economy. I have combined these topics, opportunities, and plans in the same book because they are very much interrelated and dependent on each other.

The goal of 5 percent usable fresh water will eliminate the total equivalent of all carbon emissions and pollution that the US has emitted since its inception. It will show the rest of the world how they can do the same without needing a global damage fund.

1

Achieving 5 Percent Usable Fresh Water Should Be the Top Climate Change Goal

CHAPTER 21 OF my second book, *Reject Self-Serving Power*; my third book, *Building the Climate Change Bridge*; and my fourth book, *Defeating the New Axis Powers* collectively set forth my research, analysis, conclusions, and recommendations as to why 5 percent usable fresh water should be our top climate change goal. The conclusions and recommendations thus far come about primarily through scientific and economic lenses. However, there are other reasons to select 5 percent usable fresh water as our top climate change goal. Let us discuss these matters further in this chapter.

An Exhausted Planet

The world's first water wells were invented by at least 8000 BC. These first water wells were dug by hand and often lined with stones to create a permanent wall with steps that reached down, into the water. Fire was first discovered hundreds of thousands of years ago, which started carbon emissions. Agricultural irrigation started around 6000 BC.

Roman aqueducts were first built around 312 BC and continued for five hundred years. Crude oil was first discovered in China around 600 BC and was transported in bamboo pipelines. The concept and use of sewer systems first began in Mesopotamia around 3500 BC. London developed its sewer systems around 1870 to dump human waste into the ocean. Humans are hunters and gatherers. For thousands of years, humans have been consuming the planet's natural resources. Since the formation of villages, humans have also been altering the planet's landscape to suit and build their habitats.

Our planet is rapidly approaching its point of exhaustion. As a species, a global community, and individual nations, we must stop building infrastructures that take from the planet. We must build an infrastructure that adds back to the planet instead. This infrastructure must become a permanent part of the planet.

We have a history of permanently altering the planet in modern times. The Suez Canal was built over a ten-year period in 1859–1869. First envisioned by Vasco Balboa in 1513, the Panama Canal was also built over a ten-year period in 1904–1914. Building the infrastructure for achieving the goal of 5 percent usable fresh water would be never-ending. It must start soon but never end.

Much like constructing national highway systems, international railways, and global shipping ports, when the building stops, the add-ons and maintenance begin. Highways must be constantly maintained and often widened. Airports, once built, must be constantly maintained and modernized. But unlike planetary alterations of the past that primarily harmed and used the planet, alterations for achieving the goal of 5 percent usable fresh water will *add* to the planet. Oceans will be depolluted. Ocean coastlines will stop rising. Biodiversity loss will be stopped and reversed. Fishing stocks will be built back better than ever before. Desertification will be stopped. And most importantly, our freshwater inventories can be forever replenished. Exhaustion of the planet's resources is becoming much more of a focus in the last few years. Examples of research in this include the following articles and web pages:

- "Almost Half of Earth's Vital Signs Are Now 'Code Red', Scientists Warn"

    "Climate change is not a standalone issue," says sustainability scientist Saleemul Huq from Independent University, Bangladesh. "It is part of a larger systemic problem of ecological overshoot where human demand is exceeding the regenerative capacity of the biosphere."[1]
- "Humanity Uses 70% More of the Global Commons Than the Earth Can Regenerate"[2]
- "The Nine Planetary Boundaries"[3]
- "Planet Earth: 8 Billion People and Dwindling Resources"

    The UN estimates that the global human population will reach 8 billion by mid-November. Experts say overconsumption of the planet's resources is a bigger problem than overpopulation.[4]

Providing Hope for a Great Future

It is no secret that younger generations around the world are growing increasingly pessimistic and apathetic about their futures. Who can blame them? I have found that people everywhere are desperate for strategy and leadership. They want to believe in something better and to understand and believe in destinies that matter. Consider the following:

- "Young People Are Anxious about Climate Change and Say Governments Are Failing Them"

    How are young people coping with climate change? The answer, according to one study, is not well, and for good reason.[5]
- "Majority of Young American Adults Say Climate Change Influences Their Decision to Have Children"

    Seventy-five percent of Gen Zers and 77% of millennials said climate change has affected their major life decisions, according to new research. The survey of 2,000 Americans, split evenly by four generations, revealed 78% of Gen

Zers aren't planning—or didn't want—to have children of their own as a result of climate change. Seven in 10 millennials felt the same—but that's not all: In addition to their thoughts on parenthood, 50% of Gen Zers said their career path changed due to climate change. And 73% of millennials say climate change affected where they planned to live.

It hasn't only affected their decisions—it's also impacting their health, as results revealed climate change has negatively affected 59% of respondents' mental health (71% for millennials and 67% for Gen Z).[6]

- "Gen Z Is Increasingly Developing Anxiety about Climate Change"

  With the rise of natural disasters and increasing concerns related to climate change, many young people are feeling the effects of eco-anxiety—a persistent worrying related to the future of the planet and its inhabitants.

  In fact, a recent survey shows that about 83% of Gen Z Americans—people between the ages of 14 and 24—are concerned about the health of the planet and say that the quality of their environment affects their health and well-being. For one in three, an environmental event or natural disaster—not including COVID-19—prevented them from being able to exercise outside at least once in the past five years. A fourth of all respondents also said that a similar event impacted their ability to concentrate in school.[7]

Immediate Economic Payback Clears the Thirty-Year Mortgage Test Hurdle

My biggest frustration with net-zero carbon is its total and reckless disregard for near-term economic reality. When considering any strategy for solving climate change, I always look at what I call the thirty-year mortgage test. (See NASA's discussion on this same data point in chapter

1.) If any climate change strategy does not have at least some tangible and measurable economic return within thirty years, then that strategy is essentially worthless. I derived this test from mortgage lenders.

Imagine you are trying to get a thirty-year mortgage for an oceanfront property. If the lender cannot see a path that is clear of climate change impacts over those thirty years, you will not get the mortgage. In practice, it gets worse. The timelines for trying to keep valid insurance get shorter. If the lender cannot see the property obtaining insurance for the full term of the loan, the loan will also likely be rejected. If you live in Florida, you are already painfully aware of the difficulties involved in getting insurance for coastline properties. The benefits of net-zero carbon in a hundred years or longer are essentially useless in our real lives.

I recently spoke on this topic with a senior commercial loan officer from Florida who was employed by a top-five bank. The conversation included details of their recent closing on a large-property commercial mortgage on the coast. The customer received only one insurance quote at an amount a few times greater than they'd expected. The bank's position was that the customer could accept the quote or forget the loan. Needless to say, they took the quote.

This painful lesson is growing prevalent. In not many years, you will not be able to get a thirty-year mortgage for coastal residential or commercial properties, because there is a growing concern in the banking industry that at some point during the life of the loan, the customer will have their property insurance canceled or not renewed due to rising ocean coastlines. The property values of coastal real estate will be devastated.

Conversely, if the nation adopts the goal of 5 percent usable fresh water, insurance actuaries will be able to at least build insurance rates with a coastline-rise discount factor. Although it will likely be very small in the beginning, it is at least includable in their actuarial tables. Furthermore, the amount of the actuarial value will rise in a direct relationship to the amount of the nation's adoption of and investment in the goal of 5 percent usable fresh water. As an example, let us assume that the US federal and all necessary state governments formally endorsed the goal and signed legislation to begin digging ten climate change lakes. Then the actuarial tables could include the amount of ocean water expected to be piped inland. That imported water could be translated to its commensurate reduction in rising global ocean coastlines.

As more countries adopt and implement their own plans, the actuarial tables would become more reliable. Even better, all this would happen before any money was spent on digging the first climate change lakes and building the pipelines. After construction of pipelines begins, the long-term benefits will quickly rise. See the following excerpts:

> Climate issue: The cost of comprehensive cover could become exorbitant, even as it is needed more than ever.[8]

> Mortgage lenders and investors are woefully unprepared not only to mitigate their risk but to even gauge that risk, according to a new report from the Mortgage Bankers Association's Research Institute for Housing America. "They are anxious to figure out what to do but not sure where to go to find out. They are unprepared but no longer unaware," said Sean Becketti, author of the report and former chief economist at Freddie Mac. There are numerous stakeholders in housing finance, including consumers, landlords, homebuilders, appraisers, mortgage originators and servicers, insurance companies, mortgage investors, government agencies, and the government-sponsored enterprises that issue mortgages (Fannie Mae and Freddie Mac). That means climate change will send significant pressure down a long financial line. Not only is climate change putting more stress on the National Flood Insurance Program, it could increase mortgage default and prepayment risks, trigger adverse selection in the types of loans that are sold to the GSEs, increase the volatility of house prices,

and produce significant climate migration, according to the report.[9]

Climate change is starting to transform the classic home loan, a fixture of the American experience and financial system that dates back generations. Up and down the coastline, rising seas and climate change are transforming a fixture of American homeownership that dates back generations: the classic 30-year mortgage. And in one of the clearest signs that banks are worried about global warming, they are increasingly getting these mortgages off their own books by selling them to government-backed buyers like Fannie Mae, where taxpayers would be on the hook financially if any of the loans fail. "Conventional mortgages have survived many financial crises, but they may not survive the climate crisis," said Jesse Keenan, an associate professor at Tulane University. "This trend also reflects a systematic financial risk for banks and the U.S. taxpayers who ultimately foot the bill." If climate change makes coastal homes uninsurable, Dr. Becketti wrote, their value could fall to nothing, and unlike the 2008 financial crisis, "homeowners will have no expectation that the values of their homes will ever recover." In 30 years from now, if global-warming emissions follow their current trajectory, almost half a million existing homes will be on land that floods at least once a year, according to data from Climate Central, a research organization. Those homes are valued at $241 billion.[10]

Long-Term Economic Gains

The long-term economic gains from the goal of 5 percent usable fresh water will be enormous and unprecedented. Chapter 12 will provide an in-depth discussion on this subject.

Politically Viable and Consensus Enabling Strategy

There is no sense in trying to sugar coat it—the green energy rollout in the US has been a disaster. This disaster was entirely inevitable. Green energy public policy is in shambles and basically nonexistent. Another beauty of the goal of 5 percent usable fresh water is that no matter what green-energy camp you believe in, you cannot credibly dispute this goal and its short- and long-term benefits.

Best Weapon against Inflation—Destroying Global Economies

The global and national wars on fossil fuels have created massive inflation across the planet. The US Federal Reserve and their equivalent organizations worldwide have all had to respond by raising interest rates and reducing financial liquidity in order to purposely cause recessions that fight the inflation. This is economic madness. The goal of 5 percent usable fresh water makes the wars on fossil fuels unnecessary. For more information, see the following articles:

- "The Fed Will Only Stop Tightening if There's a Recession, and Investors Are Stretching if They're Hoping for a Pivot, Citi's US Investment Strategist Warns"[11]
- "Fed Official Suggests Substantial Rate Hikes May Be Needed"[12]
- "Starwood's Barry Sternlicht Says What the Fed Is Doing to the Economy Is 'Suicide'"[13]
- "New Englanders Are Fed Up with High Energy Prices"[14]
- "Energy group issues roadmap for House Republicans to boost US energy security. Power the Future slammed what it called President Biden's 'green assault on American energy'"[15]

Megadroughts

Droughts, floods, hurricanes, and other major weather events have been part of our planet for millennia. But global warming has disrupted the planet's historical weather patterns. We can recover from floods. We can rebuild from hurricanes. But we cannot survive worsening domestic and global megadroughts. For further information, review the following articles:

- "The US Megadrought Won't Just End—It Will Change the Land Forever"[16]
- "What Is Causing the Megadroughts in North and South America?"[17]
- "Western 'Megadrought' Is the Worst in 1,200 Years."[18]
- "U.S. Droughts Will Be the Worst in 1,000 Years"[19]
- "Why Is the Mississippi River Drying Up?"[20]
- "US Megadrought Could Upend Life as We Know It—Just Look to History"[21]

Also read the following excerpts:

> Climate change is a significant factor, UCLA-led research finds. The drought that has enveloped southwestern North America for the past 22 years is the region's driest "megadrought"—defined as a drought lasting two decades or longer—since at least the year 800.[22]

> The megadrought that has plagued the West for several decades is not only expected to persist, but drought conditions will also likely intensify and expand east, according to the National Oceanic and Atmospheric Administration. About 55% of the continental U.S. is experiencing drought conditions, which will likely worsen in the Great Plains, particularly the central and southern Plains, such as Texas and Oklahoma, NOAA scientists said during a monthly climate call Thursday.[23]

> We now have enough observations of current drought and tree-ring records of past drought to say that we're on the same trajectory as the worst prehistoric droughts.[24]

Water is growing more scarce due to climate change. Water scarcity could derail the green energy boom, and even hinder fossil fuel production. With rising concerns over water scarcity, mainly due to climate change, there are fears that the big transition to renewable energy will be hindered even further.[25]

Drought conditions are worsening in the U.S., and that is having an outsized impact on the real estate that houses the internet. Data centers generate massive amounts of heat through their servers because of the enormous amount of power they use. Water is the cheapest and most common method used to cool the centers. In just one day, the average data center could use 300,000 gallons of water to cool itself—the same water consumption as 100,000 homes, according to researchers at Virginia Tech who also estimated that one in five data centers draws water from stressed watersheds mostly in the west. "There is, without a doubt, risk if you're dependent on water," said Kyle Myers, vice president of environmental health, safety & sustainability at CyrusOne, which owns and operates over 40 data centers in North America, Europe, and South America. "These data centers are set up to operate 20 years, so what is it going to look like in 2040 here, right?"[26]

When people use freshwater beyond a physically sustainable rate, it sets off a cascade of impacts on ecosystems, people, and the planet. These impacts include groundwater wells running dry, fish populations becoming stranded before they are able to spawn and protected wetland ecosystems turning into dry landscapes. We identified 168 basins across the world that are the most likely to experience social and ecological impacts due to insufficient freshwater availability. These hotspot basins are found on every continent—a clear indication of the widespread, global nature of these challenges.[27]

Controlling Flooding

The flip side of megadroughts is flooding. Climate change lakes could be used to trap and retain fresh water that sometimes appears in deserts. Unfortunately, these desert flood waters normally run off quickly because no vegetation is available to stop the flooding. If a country's terrain allows, it may be possible to dig climate change lakes in nondesert areas to control those areas' floods—such as Pakistan, which has massive flooding. For more information, read the article "Equilibrium/Sustainability—A Rainy Future for the Desert Southwest" from *The Hill*.[28]

Inland Freshwater Climate-Change Lakes and Mountains

The strategy of digging inland climate-change lakes and resulting mountains can also be used in countries that are experiencing dramatic flooding, like Ghana and Pakistan. This is a vertical strategy that could help make those countries' geographies, climates, fisheries, forests, and other natural resources better than ever.

Growing Understanding and Capitulation That Net-Zero Carbon and Paris Agreement Have No Chance of Success

There is a growing understanding and capitulation around the world that net-zero carbon and the Paris Agreement have no chance of success—at least not in this century. Perhaps in the next century, they can succeed but not in the twenty-first. Examples of this growing understanding and capitulation are included in the following excerpts:

> "The continuing rise in concentrations of the main heat-trapping gases, including the record acceleration

in methane levels, shows that we are heading in the wrong direction," said WMO Secretary-General Petteri Taalas."[29]

Breakthrough Energy Ventures, the climate-technology investment firm started by Microsoft co-founder Bill Gates, will begin to devote more to companies that help people and businesses adapt to the consequences of climate change. "It's time to start accepting reality and that we're not going to be able to do this fast enough, the ship is too big, it's too hard to steer," Eric Toone, one half of the investing committee for Breakthrough Energy Ventures (BEV), told conference attendees last week. Toone highlighted a quote from John Holdren, a research professor at Harvard University who served as President Obama's science advisor: "We basically have three choices: mitigation, adaptation and suffering." "We're left with adaptation," Toone told the audience. "And so while BEV's principal focus will continue to be mitigation, we will now work on adaptation as part of our portfolio—adaptation to some of the most severe consequences of elevated levels of greenhouse gases and global warming."[30]

United Nations Chief Antonio Guterres has warned world leaders gathered at the COP27 climate summit in Egypt that humanity faces a stark choice between working together or "collective suicide" in the battle against global warming. Nearly 100 heads of state and government are meeting in the Red Sea resort of Sharm el-Sheikh, facing calls to deepen emissions cuts and financially back developing countries already devastated by the effects of rising temperatures.

"Humanity has a choice: cooperate or perish," Guterres told the summit on Monday. "It is either a climate solidarity pact or a collective suicide pact," Guterres said, urging richer polluting nations to come to the aid of poorer countries least responsible for the emission of heat-trapping gases. Current trends would see carbon pollution increase 10 percent by the end of the decade and Earth's surface heat up by 2.8C (5F). Despite decades of climate talks—the Egypt COP is the 27th Conference of the Parties—progress has been insufficient to save the planet from excessive warming as countries are too slow or reluctant to act, he noted. "Greenhouse gas emissions keep growing. Global temperatures keep rising. And our planet is fast approaching tipping points that will make climate chaos irreversible," he said. "We are on a highway to climate hell with our foot still on the accelerator."[31]

New research published in the Journal Nature shows extensive thinning of Greenland's ice sheet and a speedup of the Northeast Greenland Ice Stream that drains glacier ice into the sea. The ice stream deterioration could raise sea levels by as much as 15.5mm (0.6 inch)—more than six times what scientists had previously estimated. According to the research, the speedup of the NEGIS will cause sea level rise by 2100 equivalent to the contribution of the entire Greenland ice sheet over the past 50 years.[32]

If the United States is to reach its 2050 decarbonization goals, the US economy might need to increase its electricity generation capacity by as much as 480% to comply with the Paris Accords.[33]

Fresh data released at the climate summit show global carbon dioxide emissions from fossil fuels are soaring despite energy crisis. Global carbon dioxide emissions from fossil fuels are projected to increase 1% in 2022, hitting a new record of 37.5 billion tonnes, scientists announced today at the United Nations Climate Change Conference of the Parties (COP27) in Sharm El-Sheikh, Egypt. If the trend continues, humanity could pump enough CO_2 into the atmosphere to warm Earth to 1.5 °C above pre-industrial temperatures in just nine years. The 2015 Paris climate agreement set this aspirational limit, seeking to avoid the most serious consequences for the planet.

"Nine years is not very long," says Corinne Le Quéré, a climate scientist at the University of East Anglia in Norwich, UK, and a member of the Global Carbon Project, which conducted the analysis. There is clearly no sign of the kind of decrease that is needed to meet international goals, she says, and even with aggressive action, climate models suggest the world is likely to at least temporarily cross the 1.5 °C threshold sometime in the 2030s.[34]

New results show average sea level rise approaching the 1-foot mark for most coastlines of the contiguous U.S. by 2050. The Gulf Coast and Southeast will see the most change. By 2050, sea level along contiguous U.S. coastlines could rise as much as 12 inches (30 centimeters) above today's waterline, according to researchers who analyzed nearly three decades of satellite observations. The results from the NASA Sea Level Change Team could help refine near-term projections for coastal communities that are bracing for increases in both catastrophic and nuisance flooding in coming years.

Global sea level has been rising for decades in response to a warming climate, and multiple lines of evidence indicate the rise is accelerating. The new findings support the higher-range scenarios outlined in an interagency report released in February 2022. That report, developed by several federal agencies—including NASA, the National Oceanic and Atmospheric Administration (NOAA), and the U.S. Geological Survey—expect significant sea level rise over the next 30 years by region. They projected 10 to 14 inches (25 to 35 centimeters) of rise on average for the East Coast, 14 to 18 inches (35 to 45 centimeters) for the Gulf Coast, and 4 to 8 inches (10 to 20 centimeters) for the West Coast. Building on the methods used in that earlier report, a team led by scientists at NASA's Jet Propulsion Laboratory in Southern California leveraged 28 years of satellite altimeter measurements of sea surface height and correlated them with NOAA tide gauge records dating as far back as 1920. By continuously measuring the height of the surrounding water level, tide gauges provide a consistent record to compare with satellite observations. The researchers noted that the accelerating rate of sea level rise detected in satellite measurements from 1993 to 2020—and the direction of those trends—suggest future sea level rise will be in the higher range of estimates for all regions. The trends along the U.S. Southeast and Gulf coasts are substantially higher than for the Northeast and West coasts, although the range of uncertainty for the Southeast and Gulf coasts is also larger. This uncertainty is caused by factors such as the effects of storms and other climate variability, as well as the natural sinking or shifting of Earth's surface along different parts of the coast.

"A key takeaway is that sea level rise along the U.S. coast has continued to accelerate over the past three decades," said JPL's Ben Hamlington, leader of the NASA Sea Level Change Team and a co-author of both the new study and the earlier report. Hamlington noted that the team wanted to determine if they could refine sea level estimates for communities facing imminent changes. "We've been hearing from practitioners and planners along the coasts that they need more information on shorter timescales—looking not 70 or 80 years into the future, but looking 20 or 30 years into the future," he said. "The bottom line is that when looking ahead to what we might experience in coming years, we need to consider these higher possibilities."[35]

Also review the following articles and web pages:

- "World 'Nowhere Near' Hitting Climate Targets, U.N. Warns"[36]
- "The Paris Agreement Is Failing; We Need a New Approach"[37]
- "G7 Firms Failing Paris Agreement on 2.7°C Warming Path"[38]
- "Not a Single G20 Country Is in Line with the Paris Agreement on Climate, Analysis Shows"[39]
- "Paris Climate Agreement: Instead of Regulations and Mandates, Embrace Markets"[40]
- "The Energy Transition Will Fail Unless Industry Fixes Wind Power Issues, Siemens Energy CEO Says"[41]
- "Confusion, Finger-Pointing, Opposing Views at Egypt's COP27"[42]
- "Electric Vehicles Are Less Reliable Because of Newer Technologies, Consumer Reports Finds"[43]

Best Path Forward for Helping Developing Countries' Global Warming Transition

There is growing pressure on the richer countries to help developing countries deal with and pay for their climate change needs. The goal of 5 percent usable fresh water is, by far, the best strategy to serve this need. For more information, read the article "Investors Have Trillions to Fight Climate Change. Developing Nations Get Little of It" from NPR.[44]

> At the two-week United Nations Climate Change Conference of the Parties (COP27) in Egypt, financing for "loss and damage" is on the agenda for the first time. This is a landmark: after decades, high emitters are finally hearing the demand that they compensate low- and middle-income countries (LMICs) for the effects of climate change that many are already feeling. Now all parties must proceed with care, build on research, study other UN environment negotiations, and discuss their positions in a constructive spirit of give and take. The need for loss-and-damage finance can no longer be denied.[45]

Creating hundreds of millions of acres of new farmlands, forests, and abundant fresh water to stop desertification and support livestock would be the best way to help developing nations deal with climate change. Review the following articles:

- "Livestock is a form of climate justice in the Global South"[46]
- "Protesters Call for Compensation from Wealthy Nations at COP27"[47]
- "Exxon Mobil Makes First Oil Discovery in Angola in 20 Years"[48]
- "Left-Wing Green Agenda Backed by John Kerry Would be 'Disaster' for Developing World, Experts Say"[49]
- "Biden Announces $20B to Move Indonesia Away from Coal"[50]

- "Low-Income Countries Want More Money for Climate Damage. They're Unlikely to Get It"[51]
- "Demands for 'Climate Reparations' Are Laughable"[52]

Also see the following excerpts:

> The push for major, debt-free funding for climate-vulnerable countries that have contributed little to the onset of global warming has made significant strides in recent years. Searing heat waves, hypercharged storms, rising sea levels, devastating droughts, and floods—evidence of climate change's calamitous impact is being felt from the Bahamas to Bangladesh, and it's fueling a growing movement for climate "reparations."[53]

> A draft agreement for the international COP27 climate summit includes funds for "loss and damages," a long-sought provision paying reparations to countries on the front lines of environmental disaster.[54]

> The fund will be targeted toward the most vulnerable countries, a key demand from wealthy nations that didn't want money flowing to China and other higher-income countries.[55]

> Government ministers and negotiators from nearly 200 countries finally secured an agreement Sunday to create a new fund to compensate poor nations for the "loss and damage" they're experiencing as a result of extreme weather worsened by climate change.[56]

> The issue of paying vulnerable countries for their climate losses has divided the U.S., European Union, and China during the U.N. negotiations in Egypt. The talks in Egypt set the stage for more conclusive negotiations at

the next U.N. climate summit, scheduled for late 2023 in the United Arab Emirates. Those talks will try to develop more details on the design of the new fund.[57]

Today in a long overdue decision, three decades in the making, all governments at COP27 agreed to set up a Loss and Damage Fund. This is a first step in a process to rectify the systemic injustice to billions of people, particularly in the Global South, who are the least responsible but are on the frontlines of the climate crisis. Those who are suffering devastating climate impacts; floods, droughts, hurricanes, and sea level rise, will have some hope that their right to access support will be respected. For two weeks, the G77 plus China, the largest developing country negotiation group representing over 134 countries and five billion of the world's population, have stood united and resolutely behind the demand for the creation of a fund at COP27 for addressing Loss and Damage. This despite intense pressure from countries like the USA who attempted to block the creation of a fund from the onset, and some EU nations who attempted to derail the talks with watered down options that would divide developing countries. The creation of the Loss and Damage Fund today is also a clear victory for civil society groups across the world, who made this issue a priority and used their power to put sustained pressure on rich nations to take responsibility for the crisis they have historically caused.[58]

The goal of 5 percent usable fresh water will eliminate the total equivalent of all carbon emissions and pollution that the US has ever emitted since its inception. It will also show the rest of the world how they can do the same without the need for a global damage fund.

Speed of Strategy Implementation and Direct Impacts on Rising Ocean Coastlines—Not Just Hoping for Indirect Impacts

One of the biggest weaknesses of the Paris Agreement and net-zero carbon is not directly taking on rising ocean coastlines, desertification, biodiversity loss, fresh water depletion, and ocean pollution. Instead, the Paris Agreement and net-zero carbon set arbitrary goals and assume that the indirectness of it all will amble its way to direct impacts. But all this is just wishful thinking.

In contrast, the goal of 5 percent usable fresh water directly targets immediately stopping rising ocean coastlines. Impacts on desertification can be immediately forecasted. Direct timelines for filtering and remediating ocean dead zones can be projected with relative certainty from the outset. Direct and positive impacts on global and domestic insurance markets will happen immediately after adopting a plan by federal, state, and local municipal authorities. Firming up insurance markets will, in turn, shore up lending and banking for coastal real estate.

Go on Offense and Stop Just Playing Defense

There is an old saying in American football that the best defense is a great offense. Net-zero carbon and the Paris Agreement are exclusively defensive strategies. It seems like saying, "We basically have three choices: mitigation, adaptation, and suffering." They are both entirely defensive strategies.

I do not accept that these are our only possibilities or choices. I reject using an entirely defensive strategy. I say let us go on offense. Keep the defense, and make it even better, but do not just leave it up to defense to win the game. We must go on offense.

The goal of 5 percent usable fresh water is a strategy built on offense. It is not constrained by the planet being inherited by early Homo sapiens and Neanderthals. The goal of 5 percent usable fresh water will forever change the planet in ways that make it better than it has ever been.

2

Positioning Climate Change Lakes, Islands, and Serendipity Pools in North America

Climate Change Lakes in North America

IT IS BEYOND the scope of this book to establish the precise location plans for the chain of climate change lakes. Those plans will need to be developed through combined planning sessions with federal, state, and local authorities. However, I will offer a potential framework to begin the conversations and plans for a chain of climate change lakes in North America.

Five Deserts of North America

North America has five major desert areas, which include several smaller well-known deserts. The Great Basin Desert is centrally located in northern Nevada and includes parts of eastern Oregon, southern Idaho, and western Utah. The Painted Desert is primarily located in southeast Utah and northern Arizona. This is the easternmost desert in the US. The Mojave Desert is located in southern Nevada and southeastern California. The Sonoran Desert is primarily located in southern Arizona.

Finally, the Chihuahuan Desert is located primarily in northern Mexico, but it reaches into southwest Texas and southern New Mexico.

> "Water is now a valuable asset for us, and as it becomes more scarce, the more we will fight to make sure we have enough," a cartel operative told VICE World News. URIQUE, Mexico—Deep inside a canyon in the mountains of Chihuahua, Mexico—a place that's accessible only by mule or on foot—locals haven't seen this river full for over eight years. And now, the waterway is the property of the Sinaloa Cartel. "Here, everything has an owner," said a mid-level Sinaloa Cartel commander for the region, who asked to be called "El Señor." "Rivers, creeks, lakes … everything, and especially water." During what Mexican authorities called the worst drought in the country's history last year, thousands of local farmers— many of them Indigenous Raramuri people—lost their crops. But the Sinaloa Cartel saw a new business opportunity: the control and distribution of water. Using water trucks, pipelines, and an army of lookouts, the cartel is siphoning water from lakes, rivers, and creeks in the mountains of the northern state of Chihuahua. The business model is twofold: The cartel wants to keep its own weed and poppy fields irrigated, and it wants to be the broker that supplies water to farmers, hotels, and other local businesses that have been left dry. "Water is now a valuable asset for us, and as it becomes more scarce, the more we will fight to make sure we have enough," El Señor said.[59]

Also read the article "Mexico Releases 'Ambitious' Renewable Energy Targets to Fight Climate Change" from Yahoo News.[60]

A high-level diagram of the five North American deserts and the geographical optics for the goal of 5 percent usable fresh water are presented in figure 1.

<u>Figure 1</u>

Deserts of North America
WA
OR
ID
Great Basin
Ogallala Aquifer
CA
NV
UT
Methane & Dust Super Emitter Oil Fields
Mojave
Painted
AZ
NM
Sonoran
TX
Baja
Chihuahuan
Gulf of California
Gulf of Mexico
Mexico
= Climate Change Lake Pipeline Entry Point for Importing Ocean Salt Waters

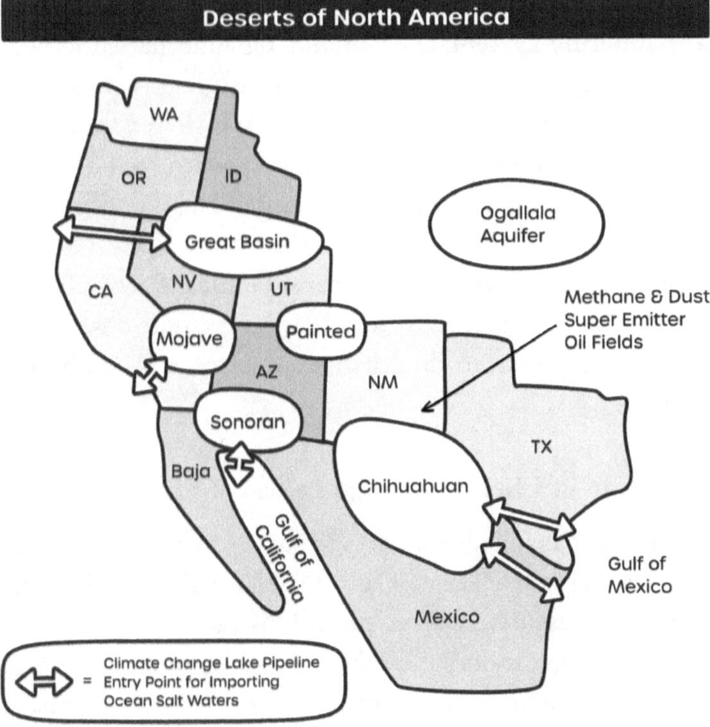

Ocean Saltwater Pipeline Import Points

Figure 1 shows five ocean saltwater pipeline import points. Two pipeline import points come in from the Gulf of Mexico, two from the Pacific Ocean, and one from the Gulf of California. This results in three import points coming into the US and two coming into Mexico. There is redundancy built into the import points and systems to enhance speed and create operating redundancy for the future.

Inland Water Pipeline Systems

Primary pipeline system. The inland pipeline networks would be designed to connect all five North American deserts to one other, so both salt and desalinated fresh water can be transferred from desert area to desert area as needed. Both natural and constructed elevations will be used within the networks for the potential creation of hydroelectric power as the pipeline system is built.

Secondary desalinated freshwater pipelines. A secondary pipeline system will also be constructed to sell and transport desalinated fresh water—potentially east, to the Mississippi River, and south, into most of Mexico.

Digging Chain of Climate Change Lakes

The plan for climate change lakes is to dig a series and chains of lakes, not just a few extremely large ones. This plan will optimize importing salt water to useless desert areas only. This plan will also bring lakes online faster because it does not rely on waiting for a few large lakes to be dug before importing salt water from the ocean entry points. We also plan to leave small, undug climate change islands within the climate change lakes while they are constructed. These islands can have many uses in the future, as discussed later in this book.

The depth and surface area of the lakes will be determined as the overall plan is prepared, analyzed, and approved by federal, state, and local authorities. The sizes, shapes, depths, altitudes, and locations of these climate change lakes can and will be very diverse to protect desired desert areas and create biodiversity havens.

Climate change lakes could be connected with a series of open, narrow—but deep—canals and trenches. These trenches could be used to create colder waters to support cold-water plants and animals such as seaweed, kelp, seals, and salmon. These designs would be included in the initial planning. For more information, read the article "The Seaweed Superfood Revolution Could End World Hunger—and Save the Planet" from *Yahoo Finance*.[61]

Geographical positioning and digging directions can meander around the deserts. This would keep and maintain desired desert and rock formations but also use useless desert areas.

Long-Term Plans

These climate change lakes will be built over a decade or more and can be enhanced over the coming centuries. Much like building the interstate highway system, digging and enhancing the climate change lakes will never stop. Each enhancement will benefit future generations and leave the planet more healed and healthier than ever before.

Climate Change Lakeside Footprints and Infrastructures

Each of the five desert areas will have at least one desalination facility and power utility (e.g., floating solar, nonfloating solar, wind, geothermal, hydroelectric, nuclear).

Shoreline properties will include multiple sand beachfronts; luxury and nonluxury residential shorefront units for both single-family homes and high-rise condos; industrial shorefronts for things like fisheries, marine research, and shipbuilding; and shoreline recreational buildings (e.g., marinas, hotels, and restaurants).

Around the shorelines will be "first circle" properties. These properties will include additional residential and commercial communities. Then, moving ever further away, will be second, third, and fourth circle properties. These properties would include agricultural industries and infrastructures (e.g., farms and processing plants) and mountains built from digging the climate change lakes. These mountains will be further discussed in chapter 5. Review the article "Washington to Prohibit Commercial Finfish Net Pen Aquaculture from State's Waters" from *KOMO News.*[62]

Underneath the previously mentioned infrastructures, we would build a network of underground saltwater and freshwater pipelines to connect saltwater distributions among the desert areas and to distribute and sell desalinated fresh water to regions elsewhere.

> There is an urgent need to explore alternative water storage solutions. Two-thirds of global cropland depends on rainfall and often makes up for its absence by using non-sustainable water resources, such as non-renewable groundwater, or impeding environmental flows.[63]

Climate Change Islands in North America

A comprehensive plan to build climate change islands in North America is also beyond the scope of this book. However, a possible starting place could be built around both the Florida Keys and islands in the Caribbean. Another interesting starting plan could be to add acreage to Guantanamo Bay. Guantanamo Bay would then become a residential and commercial haven for building the Caribbean and promoting democracy in Cuba. The eventual outcome would be a free and democratic Cuba. Review the following articles:

- "Half World's Birds in Decline, Species Moving 'Ever Faster' to Extinction"[64]
- "People Are Fleeing Puerto Rico, Guam and Every Other U.S. Territory. What Gives?"[65]
- "Study Warns of Climate Change's Looming Devastation of Insect Species"[66]
- "Coral Restoration Goes Big"[67]

3

Open Ocean and Glacier Water Chillers

IN CHAPTER 1, we discussed the fundamental issue that net-zero carbon and the Paris Agreement do not really target specific outcomes or events that cause climate change. The absolute worst hot spots are treated with the same weight as the other end of the climate change spectrum. In our strategy to obtain 5 percent usable fresh water are specifically targeted hot spots for climate change, pollution, and carbon emissions. This is just basic decision making, right? Let us start defeating climate change and global warming by prioritizing our decisions, actions, and desired outcomes.

The first hot-point area we will target is the Gulf of Mexico. In chapter 2, we discussed our plans to import salt water from the Gulf of Mexico through two separate import points. One of the reasons we are targeting the Gulf of Mexico is because it is one of the largest ocean dead zones on the planet. We also plan to target the Gulf of Mexico to try to reduce its water temperature, especially during traditional hurricane seasons.

Our goal is to simply lessen the impacts of hurricanes in the Gulf, as preventing them entirely is impossible. We are trying to develop a plan that could reduce the category of a hurricane, which would reduce its impact inland. For example, if we could reduce a category 5 to a category 4.5, we could see a big reduction in losses inland.

In order to accomplish a reduction in Gulf water temperatures, we are currently evaluating the potential of immersing industrial chillers directly into the hot points prior to a hurricane. These chillers would be powered by floating solar, nonfloating solar, or wind energy stations. We also have plans for other uses of industrial chillers in fighting global warming and climate change to rebuild mountain glaciers. More information on this will be provided in chapter 4.

Thus far, we have only experimented with off-the-shelf chillers. If we can demonstrate efficacy in using chillers to reduce targeted ocean temperatures and rebuild mountain glaciers, we could presumably increase efficacy with custom-built chillers that are much larger.

Chiller Drone Ships and Submarines

If the use of industrial chillers proves successful in cooling ocean hot points, fleets of customized drone surface ships and submarines could be constructed to target ocean hot points and protect those surface areas. Examples could include the following:

- drone ships that patrol Caribbean hot points during hurricane season;
- hurricane pathways, which would steer the hurricanes a few degrees away from heavily populated areas;
- drone-chiller submarines that protect kelp forests;
- drone-chiller submarines that cool waters at the poles, specifically major breakup points; and
- drone surface-chiller ships that create snow and ice around both poles' shrinking ice masses.

4

Rebuilding Mountain Range Snowcaps and Glaciers

IN CHAPTER 3, we began discussing how we might evaluate the potential use of industrial chillers. Perhaps these chillers could also be used to rebuild mountaintop snowcaps and glaciers. Rebuilding mountain snowcaps and mountain glaciers is very much a part of achieving the goal of 5 percent usable fresh water. As an important reminder, achieving our goal will require us to desalinate salt water and transfer that new fresh water inland.

It is common knowledge that current snowcaps and glaciers are melting due to global warming. Those melting snowcaps and ice contribute to more flooding, because the snow is melting faster and sooner than it has in the past. Droughts are then occurring, because those snowcaps have already melted and been sent to the open oceans. If we can rebuild those snowcaps and glaciers, we could reduce flooding, droughts, and rising ocean coastlines by keeping the waters inland. Presumably we could also have an impact by lowering atmospheric temperatures; although, we have no evidence that would occur.

We plan to rebuild existing snowcaps and build new ones by creating new mountains from the land dug during the creation of the climate change lakes. The physical structures necessary to rebuild old and build new snowcaps will include traditional snow-making machines that are run 24/7. The water used to create the snow will come from desalinated water. Industrial chillers will expand the snow, creating a longer cold season and slowing the melting process. Chillers will be powered by on-site solar energy systems. Fortunately, many desert areas have cold nights during much of the year.

Our belief is that the more snow we can create, the more natural snowcap processes will rebuild layers and help advance their depth. This is, by design, both a long- and short-term strategy. If we can only accomplish a ninety-day extension of a current snowcap melting season, we could easily make a significant reduction in an area's flooding. A ninety-day extension could also make a significant reduction in the following summer's drought impacts.

Another significant factor will be the increased volumes of fresh water that will be distributed to the mountaintops. That water will work its way down into mountain streams and groundwater in the historical snow-and-water-feeding cycle.

Building Biodiversity while Building New Snowcaps

While new mountain ranges are being built and historic snowcaps remediated, their construction plans can include creating new biodiversity wealth. For example, entirely new and permanent salmon runs could be planned—complete with salmon streams and migrations to and from the climate change lakes. The same could be done for trout, oysters, clams, shrimp, and more. This strategy has many of the advantages of current fish and seafood farms while also including open ocean advantages and characteristics. For more information, see the following excerpts:

Norwegian fjord and coastal ice represent a potential security threat, as it may cut off entire communities from the outside world.[68]

If this is correct, the contribution of ice dynamics to overall mass loss on Greenland will be larger than what current models suggest.[69]

5

Brine Mountains, Carbon Dioxide Peat Bogs, and Twenty-First-Century Monasteries

Brine Mountains

THERE ARE TWO foundational strategies that must always be followed while building the infrastructure necessary to achieve the goal of 5 percent usable fresh water. First, filter and clean ocean waters wherever possible. Second, *never* put stuff back into the oceans; keep it on the land. Almost all ocean pollution comes from land-based pollution.

One of the main pushbacks against building desalination plants today is increased salt levels that result from the desalination process and their impact on surrounding ocean waters. Desalination of climate change lakes will include provisions for brine drying beds. These drying beds will allow salt and forever pollutants to be extracted and captured. The residual salts, microplastics, and other forever pollutants will be added to and permanently stored in the newly created mountains. Over time, these brine mountains could be layered with compost and top soils to create layers of healthy habitats for mountain forests and other vegetation.

Cleansing Microplastics, Forever Chemicals, and Other Permanent Pollution from the Oceans

After we achieve the goal of 5 percent usable fresh water, theoretically all oceans can be cleansed of permanent pollutants and contaminants that came from human use on land. Read "California Sues 3M, DuPont over 'Forever Chemicals'" from the *Wall Street Journal*.[70]

Carbon Dioxide Peat Bogs

Many technologies and business models are being developed to extract carbon directly from the atmosphere. Where and how to store the resulting carbon is a major issue in this process. Some are even contemplating using oceans to "store" the captured carbon. Another part of the carbon-storage puzzle is the fact that crude oil drillers can and want to use captured carbon to enhance the oil-well-drilling process. This practice is rejected by net-zero carbon advocates because it extends the use of fossil fuels.

Under our goal of 5 percent usable fresh water, fossil fuels are not the enemy. Instead, they continue to be a major part of the overall energy and hydrocarbon industries. Accordingly, part of our overall plans include determining if carbon dioxide peat bogs could be created from both ocean and atmospheric extracted carbon. These captured carbons would theoretically be stored in peat bogs and used later by oil well drillers.

A key tactic here is to only extract carbon from ocean waters but never put carbon into ocean waters. Again, we must stop using the oceans as de facto dumping grounds.

Superfund Pollution Cleanup and Storage Sites

If desired, one or more of the climate change lakes could be used as a superfund pollution cleaner and storage site. Cleaning up past coal mines and surface mining sites of all kinds could be included. See the article "The Tiny Insurance Company Standing between Taxpayers and a Costly Coal Industry Bailout" from *Yahoo Financial*.[71]

Twenty-First-Century Monasteries

Many monasteries were built in Europe during the fifth and sixth centuries. These monasteries were built over decades by dedicated groups of individuals and became their homes, businesses, and places of worship and meaning. As we will discuss in later chapters of this book, tens of millions of US citizens are searching for hope, meaning, and a home.

Our plans include recruiting populations to build the equivalent of ancient monasteries in the twenty-first and twenty-second centuries. The residents of these future monasteries will be dedicated to building the new mountain ranges to help save the planet.

6

Positioning Climate Change
Lakes, Islands, and Serendipity
Pools outside North America

IF WE CAN successfully demonstrate the viability of having 5 percent usable fresh water in North America, it will become a no-brainer to export this goal to the rest of the world. A few of the targets could include climate change lakes in the Sahara Desert and Patagonia Desert, the Mediterranean Sea area, the Middle East, and Australia. It could also include climate change islands that extend the Hawaiian Islands, Midway Island, Wake Island, Guam, and the Islands of Japan.

Building climate change lakes and climate change islands in those regions would eliminate the need to compensate poor nations for climate change. This has been a festering issue under net-zero carbon. For more information, read the articles "COP27: Delegates Weigh 'Climate Compensation' for Poor Nations Impacted by Global Warming" from *Fox News* and "Guyana's Offshore Drilling Bonanza Is Just Getting Started" from *Oil Price*.[72]

7

Ocean Water Transfer Credits

AN ENTIRE INDUSTRY is being created to extract carbon from the atmosphere. One of the economic factors driving carbon extraction is the concept and creation of an asset class to trade these extracted carbons as carbon credits. These carbon credits are then purchased by commercial companies of all kinds and used to implement their own sustainability goals.

While we appreciate the concept of extracting carbon, we struggle with the economics of this business model. There are many things that puzzle us, but perhaps the most puzzling is the discounted future value of carbon transfer credits. You never hear any net-zero carbon advocate specifically say that achieving net-zero carbon will stop rising ocean coastlines, ocean pollution, desertification, biodiversity loss, or freshwater depletion. Any published works by net-zero carbon advocates will not specifically say that achieving net-zero carbon will stop those things either.

Many seem to assume this will all mysteriously happen, but we believe they are wrong. We do not believe this will all just happen—at least not in this century, and perhaps not in the next century. If we are correct, what value do carbon credits have? If you purchase something that has no value for a century or more, can you credibly claim you are achieving your sustainability goals? How can any value possibly be attributed to these "assets"?

What Are Carbon Credits?

Carbon credits, also known as carbon offsets, are permits that allow the owner to emit a certain amount of carbon dioxide or other greenhouse gases. One credit permits the emission of one ton of carbon dioxide or the equivalent in other greenhouse gases. The carbon credit is half of a so-called "cap-and-trade" program. Companies that pollute are awarded credits that allow them to continue to pollute up to a certain limit, which is reduced periodically. Meanwhile, the company may sell any unneeded credits to another company that needs them. Private companies are thus doubly incentivized to reduce greenhouse emissions. First, they must spend money on extra credits if their emissions exceed the cap. Second, they can make money by reducing their emissions and selling their excess allowances. Proponents of the carbon credit system say that it leads to measurable, verifiable emission reductions from certified climate action projects, and that these projects reduce, remove or avoid greenhouse gas (GHG) emissions.[73]

Carbon credits, often referred to as carbon allowances, can be thought of as a unit of measurement; however, they have a "tradeable" component. Carbon credits ARE NOT the same as carbon offsets. Carbon credits only exist in jurisdictions that are governed by what's called a "Cap & Trade."[74]

The trading of carbon credits can help companies—and the world—meet ambitious goals for reducing greenhouse-gas emissions. Here is what it would take to strengthen voluntary carbon markets so they can support climate action on a large scale.[75]

Ocean Water Transfer Credits

We believe a better alternative would be to trade ocean water transfer credits for ocean water transferred inland under our goal of 5 percent usable fresh water. Ocean water transfer credits will at least have a direct impact on stopping rising ocean coastlines, and perhaps most importantly, insurance actuaries and investment analysts would have the financial data points they need to forecast the price of such credits. There are no such data points to remotely price the value of carbon credits.

Building an industry and trading platform for ocean water transfer credits could start with the US and Mexican governments both passing legislation to commit to adopting the goal of 5 percent usable fresh water into law, including provisions for regulations and funding. Then private market companies—including insurance and banking—could rise to the challenge by developing and offering ocean water transfer credit products and trading mechanisms. Governments could adopt regulations that include using ocean water transfer goals to enable the launch of products and trading platforms during the construction phase. After ocean water transfers begin, governments can report daily inflows on publicly metered flow websites. Then insurers, banks, and others will use those water transfer inflows to develop actuarial projections that will estimate the impact on reducing rising ocean coastlines. Finally, oceanfront commercial and residential property owners will be able to purchase insurance and credits to insure their real estate.

8

Cleaning Up the Oceans with Climate Change Islands

BY NOW, IT should be obvious that we are obsessed with cleaning up the oceans. For centuries, humans all over the world have treated the oceans as dumping grounds and unending resources to be exploited without a thought. This must stop. Water is the key to defeating global warming and climate change. While water is the key to defeating global warming, clean and usable fresh water is the key to a healthy, habitable planet in the future.

Twenty-First-Century Monasteries on Climate Change Islands

Much like building twenty-first-century monasteries on climate change mountains—as discussed in chapter 5—we also plan to build twenty-first-century monasteries on climate change islands. Residents of climate change islands would be dedicated to cleaning up the oceans and creating habitats for rebuilding biodiversity.

Building climate change islands doesn't necessarily mean all construction must be above sea level. For example, building and expanding grassland estuaries could be a major part of this strategy. I could easily envision extending the Florida Everglades south, into the ocean—perhaps toward Cuba for approximately fifty miles. Building environments like the Galapagos Islands along the highway from Miami to the Florida Keys could restock fish populations and become tourist destinations.

Partnering with Seafloor Mining

It is only a matter of time before seafloor mining becomes a reality. The world is running out of known raw material deposits. As potentially dangerous as it is, seafloor mining will happen. Cleaning up the oceans while simultaneously mining its floors could be a symbiotic partnership to make seafloor mining palatable.

Strategically positioning climate change islands around the world would provide places to deposit the trash cleaned from the oceans. Seafloor miners partnering with climate change island builders could provide the business model that seafloor miners need to make their plans politically palatable and a net gain to the health of the oceans. For more information, read the article "North Shore Group Confronts Growing Threats of Erosion, Sea Level Rise" from *Honolulu Civil Beat*.[76]

> The mining industry is pushing to explore more of the world's deep oceans to find metals and minerals used for electric vehicles and other technologies. Scientists, lawyers, and government officials are meeting until November 11 in Jamaica to discuss the issue. The International Seabed Authority, (ISA), an independent group created by a United Nations treaty, organized the meeting. The ISA has given 31 exploration licenses for deep ocean waters outside of any country's territory. While it has not given any licenses to begin mining, some experts worry it will do so. Less than one percent of the world's deep ocean waters have been explored. Most of the current exploration activity is in a large

region between Hawaii and Mexico. The International Energy Agency estimated that demand for minerals will increase six times by 2050. A report from Fitch Ratings that was released in October said demand will increase because electric vehicles and renewable energy technologies need minerals found in the sea.[77]

Climate change and geopolitics are setting up a scramble for the global oceans. In August 2017, the survey vessel Xiang Yang Hong 06, carrying a crew of 26, departed the Chinese port of Qingdao bound for the Clarion-Clipperton Zone. The remote stretch of ocean, about 2,000 miles southeast of Baja California, contains one of the world's largest known resources of cobalt, copper, nickel and manganese.[78]

As demand for fossil fuels levels off, renewable energy sources will occupy a larger and larger percentage of the total demand for the minerals involved in their creation. Within the next two decades, the IEA predicts that renewable energy technology will make up over 40 percent of the demand for copper, 60 to 70 percent for cobalt and nickel, and 90 percent for lithium needs through a process called deep-sea mining. China, in particular, has demonstrated its desire to shape international norms in the maritime domain, as exemplified by Beijing's aggressive actions in the South China Sea and DSM. Already dominating terrestrial mining, China is now leading the race to the bottom of the sea by building superior capabilities and influencing the regulatory environment. China currently holds five out of the 30 deep-sea mining contracts issued by the ISA—more than any other country.[79]

9

Rifle Shots on Super-Emitters

NASA Super-Emitter Research

ON JULY 14, 2022, NASA launched the Earth Surface Mineral Dust Source Investigation (EMIT).

EMIT was developed at NASA's Jet Propulsion Laboratory. The instrument observes Earth from outside the International Space Station. EMIT was built to help scientists understand how dust affects climate. However, NASA soon discovered EMIT can also pinpoint emissions of the potent greenhouse gas.

EMIT's mission is mapping the prevalence of key minerals in the planet's dust-producing deserts—information that will advance our understanding of airborne dust's effects on climate. But EMIT has demonstrated another crucial capability: detecting the presence of methane, a potent greenhouse gas. In the data EMIT has collected since being installed on the International Space Station in July, the science team has identified more than 50 "super-emitters" in Central Asia, the Middle East, and the Southwestern United States. Super-emitters are facilities, equipment, and other infrastructure, typically in the fossil-fuel, waste, or agriculture sectors, that emit methane at high rates. "Reining in methane emissions is key to limiting global warming. This exciting new development will not only help researchers better pinpoint where methane leaks are coming from, but also provide insight on how they can be addressed—quickly," said NASA Administrator Bill Nelson. "The International Space Station and NASA's more than two dozen satellites and instruments in space have long been invaluable in determining changes to the Earth's climate. EMIT is proving to be a critical tool in our toolbox to measure this potent greenhouse gas—and stop it at the source." Methane absorbs infrared light in a unique pattern—called a spectral fingerprint—that EMIT's imaging spectrometer can discern with high accuracy and precision. The instrument can also measure carbon dioxide.

The new observations stem from the broad coverage of the planet afforded by the space station's orbit, as well as from EMIT's ability to scan swaths of Earth's surface dozens of miles wide while resolving areas as small as a soccer field.

"These results are exceptional, and they demonstrate the value of pairing global-scale perspective with the resolution required to identify methane point sources, down to the facility scale," said David Thompson, EMIT's instrument scientist and a senior research scientist at NASA's Jet Propulsion Laboratory in

Southern California, which manages the mission. "It's a unique capability that will raise the bar on efforts to attribute methane sources and mitigate emissions from human activities."

Relative to carbon dioxide, methane makes up a fraction of human-caused greenhouse-gas emissions, but it's estimated to be 80 times more effective, ton for ton, at trapping heat in the atmosphere in the 20 years after release. Moreover, where carbon dioxide lingers for centuries, methane persists for about a decade, meaning that if emissions are reduced, the atmosphere will respond in a similar timeframe, leading to slower near-term warming.

EMIT's initial images shows a methane plume 2 miles (3 kilometers) long that NASA's Earth Surface Mineral Dust Source Investigation mission detected southeast of Carlsbad, New Mexico. Methane is a potent greenhouse gas that is much more effective at trapping heat in the atmosphere than carbon dioxide. [80]

For more information, read the article "U.S. and EU to Crack Down on Fossil Fuel Sector's Methane Emissions" from *Oil Price*.[81]

The United Nations is launching a satellite-based system to detect and track global methane emissions as part of efforts to reduce emissions of methane, which is a more potent greenhouse gas than carbon dioxide.[82]

Dust Bowl and Methane Bogs and Mountains

The dust storm particles and methane emissions from the super-emitters could potentially be stopped while building the climate change lakes. Because NASA has located significant super-emitter sites in New

Mexico, the North American climate change lake strategy could target these super-emitters.

A potential strategy is to flood these areas with shallow climate change lakes or canals to trap the dust and methane emissions without placing any significant operating restrictions on these locations. The dust particles and methane could then be separated and stored as part of the peat bogs and mountains we previously discussed. This strategy could easily work in active oil fields, as working under shallow water conditions should not be an impediment to drilling.

10

Land Rushes of 1889, 2050, 2075, and 2100

BUILDING CLIMATE CHANGE lakes—which we will further discuss in chapter 12—will add millions of acres of habitable land, farms, and forests to our nation. This could be the largest addition of usable farm lands and forests since the Louisiana Purchase. North America has approximately 95,751 square miles of desert.[83]

We would yield approximately 32,000 square miles of new habitable and productive lands if we adopted a strategy of keeping one-third of deserts as desert; flooding one-third with climate change lakes; and then using desalinated water to allocate the final one-third for the creation of new usable residential, agricultural, and forest lands. At 640 acres per square mile, this would yield approximately 20.5 million acres.

In 1889, approximately 1.9 million acres were given away in the Oklahoma Land Rush to settlers willing to settle and live on the lands. Most of the lands created by climate change lakes will be owned by the federal, state, or local government. Much like what was done in 1889, portions of these new lands could be given away to people willing to settle and become the monasterial custodians of these new lands.

Digging the climate change lakes will also build new mountains. These new mountains will grow over time—as previously discussed. Therefore, not only will approximately 20.5 million acres of new lands be created horizontally; millions of vertical additional acres will be grown as habitable mountains, upon which habitable forests will also be created. Review the following articles:

- "Looming Food Crisis: We Need to Keep Farmland in the Hands of Farmers"[84]
- "Houston's Solution to Climate Change Is to Force Low-Income People to Move"[85]
- "The U.S. Is Running Short of Land for Housing"[86]

Also see the following excerpt:

> Compared with traditional power plants, renewable plants with the same power-generating capacity take up a lot more land: A 2017 study found that wind farms took up 70 acres per MW while solar farms required 43 acres per MW, including all the land needed for development, power generation, transportation, and storage—3 1/2 times to five times the land needed by fossil-fuel plants, respectively, according to the analysis. And where their fossil-fuel counterparts can operate all day long, wind and solar generators can operate between 20% and 35% of the time because of the intermittent nature of the energy sources.[87]

11

Maintaining and Exploiting the Positives from Global Warming

THERE ACTUALLY ARE some positives and wins surfacing as a result of global warming. However, it will take more fresh water to exploit these positives. This new requisite fresh water obviously can come from the climate change lakes. Examples include double cropping on farmlands as a result of longer growing seasons and the ability to grow citrus and other traditionally warmer-climate-grown crops in more northern regions. For more information, see the article "Greenland's Melting Ice Sheet Brings an Unexpected Flow of Wealth Potential" from *Hakai Magazine*.[88]

12

Paying for Climate Change

WHEN I THINK about developing a strategy for climate change and global warming, I think about whether or not I would propose that same strategy for solely economic reasons. I do not even consider the issues of global warming. When I look at the goal of 5 percent usable fresh water through this purely economic decision-making lens, my answer is absolutely yes.

Implementing the freshwater goal can pay for itself, pay for global warming, and pay off our nation's massive debts and unfunded Social Security and Medicare liabilities. The goal's infrastructure—as previously set forth in this book—can pay for eliminating the risk of rising ocean coastlines. It can pay for the reverse of biodiversity loss and pave the way for unprecedented gains in biodiversity for future generations. It can pay for a ten-time increase in fresh water inventories. It can pay to clean up the oceans. It can virtually eliminate destructive inflation.

As we will discuss in the following chapters, the freshwater goal can also help eliminate our nation's societal problems. Last but certainly not least, the goal can provide the centuries-long runway and bridge needed for climate change to allow green-energy technologies and shifts to cool the planet to optimal levels.

I leave it to you to prepare your own financial forecasts and capital-raising strategies. Obviously federal, state, and local governments are going to need to agree on a final framework, adopt the necessary laws, and provide seed financing. I offer the following data points and action items to kick-start these discussions.

Simply adopting a national plan to implement the goal of 5 percent usable fresh water will have an immediate positive impact on national—and likely global—hope that our economies do not need to be sacrificed to pay for climate change or global warming. Implementation will also have an immediate and positive impact on national and global insurance markets. Those, in turn, will have immediate and positive impacts on global lending for coastal real estate.

Applying an average value of approximately $5,000 per acre on the 20.5 million acres set forth in chapter 10 would imply a future raw value for the created farmlands and forestry lands. This implies a starting value of approximately $102.5 billion. Assuming a ten-time increase in value shortly after land rushes, purchases, and settlements, this would imply a near-term future value approximating $1 trillion.

The amount of climate change lake shorelines could easily exceed five thousand usable miles or 26.4 million feet of brand new oceanfront real estate. Assuming an average beginning selling price of $10,000 per oceanfront foot, this could yield real estate sales exceeding $260 billion. Applying a ten-time growth in valuation over time after settlement could yield climate change lake shoreline valuations that exceed $2.6 trillion, just for the shorefront land. Assuming that, over time, the buildings and other improvements to those shorelines approximate ten-times the land value, the total shoreline property values would likely exceed $26 trillion (to be subject to near-term future property taxes).

Assuming the federal, state, and local governments would continue to own the constructed pipelines and other infrastructure, climate change lakes, and climate change islands, these governments could derive future income taxes, and fees from at least the following:

- leases to fisheries;
- leases and/or land sales to construct and sell products and services for utilities;
- property taxes, including a federal property tax to fund Social Security, Medicare, and other social needs in the future;
- income taxes;
- sales taxes;
- land sales;
- land leases; and
- assistance to other countries outside North America who adopt their own freshwater goals and plans.

Workforce Migrations

Building and maintaining climate change lakes and islands will require domestic and foreign immigration. I could easily see each of the five desert areas recruiting and supporting ten million new residents. Climate change islands could easily recruit hundreds of thousands more. The total population shifts could easily exceed fifty million people. Assuming an average income of approximately $80,000 per person, this population shift would create an additional GDP of approximately $4 trillion annually.

All of these incremental revenues and increases in GDP do not take into consideration the opportunity costs of not pursuing the goal of 5 percent fresh water. If we do not adopt the goal, the future costs of lost oceanfront properties, increased pollution, and continued biodiversity loss and desertification will surely be in the hundreds of trillions of dollars.

History has many examples of countries immigrating, emigrating, and exiling populations for settlement and social purposes—for example, exiling prisoners to Georgia and Australia. Unforced mass migrations include the Gold Rush, Dust Bowl emigration to California, and migration to large manufacturing cities in the North to fill manufacturing facilities during World War II.

Federal, state, and local governments could literally empty their jails, prisons, homeless shelters, and other care centers by emigrating those populations to climate change lakes and islands. These people would get a fresh start in life and become productive members of society again—in many cases, for the first time in their lives. Companies that relocate operations to climate change lakes and islands could be required to include a quota of these populations in their workforce recruiting. Assume ten million people are currently at the bottom of the wealth inequality pyramid and costing governments approximately $100,000 per person. If they were emigrated, this would save government budgets approximately $1 trillion per year.

Financing Early Stage Construction and Cash Flows

Even with these amounts of future revenues and cash flows, government financing for the early stages of pipeline construction along with digging the climate change lakes would be necessary. This early stage financing would likely require the establishment of some kind of federal-asset-based lending authority, perhaps similar to GNMA and FNMA. A sunset of ten years could be established in the enabling legislation and funding. These loans could easily be repaid in the near future, as the previously discussed revenues and cash flows are built. Other potential sources of early stage financing could include the following:

- World Bank financing for Mexico to develop the Mexican part of the Chihuahuan Desert,
- state and local municipality revenue bonds,
- advance sales and deposits for land and water rights,
- advance lease deposits,
- advance and ongoing sales of desalinated fresh water, and
- advance deposits from other countries to replicate climate change lakes in their countries.

If desired, after all construction loans have been repaid, new legislation could be enacted to create ongoing fees and tax revenues to go into the general revenue category or be earmarked to pay for other governmental debts.

Costs of Digging Climate Change Lakes and Pipelines

The average cost of digging and operating a new surface mine for a period of ten years approximates $10 billion per mine, depending on the location, terrain, use purpose, and other relevant factors.[89]

Assuming it took ten years to simultaneously dig twenty chains of climate change lakes, the total cost of digging the climate change lakes would approximate $200 billion. The average cost of creating a pipeline approximates $2 million per mile.[90] If we built ten thousand miles of pipeline—including desalinated freshwater pipelines for the transportation and sale of desalinated water—the total cost for building the pipelines would approximate $20 billion. So the total construction costs for digging the climate change lakes and pipelines would approximate $220 billion.

> Utah Department of Natural Resources Executive Director Joel Ferry told the crowd that a pipeline would cost anywhere from $60-100 billion. That does not include environmental and regulatory hurdles to even make it a reality.[91]

Annual operating costs could be billed to the new land and business owners. There would also be a substantial upfront number of mining equipment purchases to make to build a fleet of surface-mining equipment. However, there is an existing fleet of used surface mining equipment available. If desired, the equipment fleet could likely be resold or re-leased to other countries after the North American climate change lakes system is built. Furthermore, equipment depreciation costs are presumably included in the previously provided cost estimates.

Simplicity of the Goal of 5 Percent Usable Fresh Water

The simplicity of the strategy for the goal of 5 percent usable fresh water is its great strength when benchmarked against net-zero carbon and the Paris Agreement. Consider the following:

> It's "now or never", one report co-chair said in releasing findings that show only drastic emissions cuts in the next few decades would keep warming from spiraling out of control. For the first time, the report's authors called for urgent action to curb methane. Up to this point, the IPCC had focused on only carbon dioxide, the most abundant greenhouse gas. With time running out, the authors said it was worth looking into the benefits and drawbacks of geoengineering, or large-scale interventions to shift the climate, such as injecting particles into the atmosphere to block out solar radiation.[92]

> The global net-zero goals set out by the Paris Agreement are still within reach—but achieving them will require a $100 trillion investment, according to a new report by BNY Mellon Investment Management and Fathom Consulting. That amount equates to around 15% of all global investment or 3% of global GDP over the next 30 years in order to achieve net zero emissions by 2050 and limit warming to 2 degrees Celsius or below, per the Paris Agreement Accord established in 2015. And the more governments, asset managers, and corporations delay, the steeper the overall price tag will be.[93]

Green Energy Economics Do Not Work

Inflation—created largely by the war on fossil fuels combined with squandering hundreds of billions (and eventually hundreds of trillions) of dollars on a net-zero carbon strategy—is destroying the very economies and working classes expected to work and pay for net-zero carbon. These combined economic wars are creating a downward economical spiral with no end but the bottom.

Conversely, the 5 percent freshwater goal creates vast new economies and wealth for all countries. Self-serving, power-driven politicians who use the war on fossil fuels to increase their power will vehemently dispute these facts. They will preach about all the new green-energy jobs that will be created. The problem with these economic arguments is the same fundamental problem that infects net-zero carbon and the Paris Agreement.

Even if all these hundreds of trillions of dollars are spent on net-zero carbon, they will be gone, and oceans will still be rising for the next century or two. Desertification will still be devastating farmlands and forests around the world. Biodiversity loss will march on, and our domestic and global freshwater inventories will continue to decline. There is no direct correlation between net-zero carbon or the Paris Agreement and the catastrophic physical events brought on by global warming—only distantly imagined, indirect outcomes that will not be realized for centuries. For more information, read the articles "The Jobs that Built America's Middle Class Are Disappearing, Intensifying Its Downfall" from *Fortune* and "Global Aquaculture Deemed to Be 'in Decline'" from *The Fish Site*.[94]

The old cliché that timing is everything is always true. Pursuing noble causes at bad times eventually makes fools of us all. Net-zero carbon by 2050 is one of those noble causes with bad timing. There is a reluctant but growing global consensus that net-zero carbon by 2050 is an impossible goal. It is time to regroup and admit that net-zero carbon is a twenty-second-century strategy. It is not a viable twenty-first-century strategy. So what do we do now? What should become our twenty-first-century destiny? What rallying point can bring us together? Fortunately, history and geography provide us with that answer.

Our twenty-first-century rallying point lies in the shifting sands of the great deserts around the world. For the most part, these deserts are owned by federal governments—primarily because nobody else wants the seemingly worthless properties. It is time to convert these historically worthless properties into the saviors of twenty-first-century climate change. My three-part series on building the climate change bridge provides the plan for cashing in these desert sands. In the United States alone, government-owned deserts could solve and pay for climate change; pay off our national debt; fund Medicare and Social Security into perpetuity; and end crime, prison life, homelessness, and wealth inequality. This is the biggest opportunity for our country since the Louisiana Purchase. It could define the United States as the guardians of the planet for all the generations and centuries to come.

13

Planning the Selfless Economy

IN MY FIRST book, *Prophecy before Vision*, and my second book, *Reject Self-Serving Power*, we discussed leadership dedicated to helping others be successful. We also discussed inverting the global wealth-inequality pyramid. I will not repeat those lessons in this book; instead, I will include these topics in the following chapters as a checklist to implement building out the infrastructure for the goal of 5 percent usable fresh water. I have added several new concepts, which are included in the following chapters. If you have not read *Prophecy before Vision* and *Reject Self-Serving Power*, you can catch up by reading our website, blogs, and newsroom at www.jmprophecies.com.

Implementing the 5 percent freshwater goal should prioritize including those people located at the bottom of the wealth-inequality pyramid when relocating workers and residents to the climate change lakes and pyramids.

14

Community Positioning for Leadership Layering and Constructing Serendipity Pools

Leadership Layering in Local Communities

ONE OF THE new tactics we are experimenting with we call *leadership layering* in communities. As discussed in my first book, everyone has the capacity to be a leader. They just need the opportunity—and sometimes some training. For example, the conventional dogma in affordable housing communities is to place the housing building in as upscale an area as possible.

We have begun to believe such buildings and populations are best served being located inside concentric villages, as discussed in my first book. These concentric villages are built around an existing jail or prison. This strategy provides the residents of the affordable housing units with the opportunities to be leaders instead of being located near the bottom of a more affluent area with no chance of leading.

Restoring Rural America

As discussed in previous chapters, we will be establishing millions of acres of new farmlands and forests as part of our strategy. These new lands will be largely rural, at least in the early years. These new lands will provide the opportunity to evaluate how rural America can be reinvigorated.

> "Rural decline is not simply the result of deindustrialization spurred by free trade, the farm crisis, or automation and robotization. Since the 1980s, financial capital has developed imaginative new ways to strip and seize the assets present in rural zones, whether these be mutually-owned banks, industries, cooperatively-owned grain elevators, local newspapers, hospitals, people's homes, or stores located in towns and malls." In the wake of the fiscal austerity agenda enacted by financial and political elites in the late 20th century, the vast majority of the wealth created in America's countryside "has accrued to shareholders in corporations and financial institutions headquartered in a handful of distant, economically dynamic urban centers." The financialization of the American economy, especially in those places furthest from economic hubs, can be extremely opaque. But its repercussions—many of which are often seen as causes and effects of backwardness and small-town decline— are all around us.[95]

Understanding Epigenetics

As discussed in my first and second books, we are interested in studying the impacts of epigenetics.

Changing the epigenetic marks on chromosomes results in altered gene expression in offspring and in grandoffspring, demonstrating "transgenerational epigenetic inheritance."

Without changing the genetic code in the DNA, epigenetic modifications can alter how genes are expressed, affecting an organism's health and development. It was once a radical idea that such changes in gene expression can be inherited. Now there is a growing body of evidence behind it, but the mechanisms involved are still poorly understood.[96]

Intelligence is determined by both your environment and your genes. As we frequently emphasize, there are a lot of things you can do to make sure your brain is always at its best, but nobody can deny that the genes you were born with make a difference too. Research into genetics has become amazingly advanced in recent years, and a new study has identified the genes involved in intelligence.[97]

Review the article "Biotech Stocks Embrace the Neuroscience Renaissance with Biogen, Amylyx at the helm" from *Investor's Business Daily*.[98]

Mental Illness

See the article "A Psychiatric Nurse Says She and Her Colleagues Are Being Pushed to a Breaking Point, and She Quit Her Dream Job Due to Violence" from *Insider*.[99]

Decision-Making under Great Uncertainty

If you have read and studied *Prophecy before Vision*, you now likely understand that it is largely about decision-making under great uncertainty. I repeat myself from my first two books—the world is becoming too complicated to live in it. We live in an era of great uncertainty, and many people are struggling with coping and living under that uncertainty. The climate change lakes and islands can provide safe havens for those populations to live healthy lives while simultaneously saving the planet. Consider the following:

> New dimensions of uncertainty are emerging. Lives are being unsettled around the world. To turn new uncertainties into opportunities, we must unleash people's creative and cooperative potential. We must double down on human development. That is the conclusion of the recently launched 2021–22 Human Development Report titled "Uncertain Times, Unsettled Lives: Shaping Our Future in a Transforming World." Feelings of insecurity are on the rise even in countries with the highest levels of HDI. At least a decade in the making, it is a trend that paralleled improvements in the HDI and other conventional measures of well-being. Likewise, reported stress levels—the feeling of being overwhelmed by what the world is throwing at us—have been increasing across all education levels.
>
> The 2021–22 Human Development Report argues that a new "uncertainty complex" is emerging, never seen before in human history. Uncertainty is not new, but its dimensions today are taking ominous new forms. Constituting it are three volatile and interacting strands:
>
> - Climate change.
> - Sweeping societal transformations.
> - Polarization among and within countries.[100]

15

Clubhouse Incubators

Building Businesses, Building Lives

AS WE DISCUSSED in my second book and repeated on our website, JM Prophecies only invests in real estate that nobody wants. We are especially looking to invest in real estate that is either adjacent to current prisons or jails or in an actual vacant prison. When we think about real estate, the next step above prisons and jails is various forms of affordable housing.

I recently met with a 501(c)(3) real estate partner who manages HUD properties. This partner conducts financial counseling classes for their tenants in a ninety-unit property. They typically get only two residents who attend their classes. This story is indicative of other experiences we have seen. As a result, we are experimenting with ideas to answer how we can help low-income (or zero-income) folks tap into higher-income-enabling knowledge.

Clubhouse Incubators

We have decided to focus on establishing technology and business incubators in prisons and jails, next to prisons and jails, and in the lowest-income areas. We start with virtual technology incubators. We call these *clubhouse incubators* because we plan to eventually locate these incubators inside apartment and single-family-home residential communities. We intend to launch technology incubators over the next few years, launching one new technology incubator per year beginning in 2024. These incubators include or will address autonomous devices, climate change, synthetic biologics and advanced polymers, epigenetics, onshoring from China, and quantum information technology and science.

As you think about this chapter, keep in mind that our target markets always begin with people mired down at the absolute bottom of the wealth-inequality pyramid—those who have no money, no job, no home, no hope, and nowhere to go. Those with absolutely nothing. So how could we possibly believe we could build these highly advanced technology incubators with those people as our target markets?

This question paves the way for our family's and our company's quest and dives to the heart of our most-fundamental scientific belief. That scientific belief is the power of nature's self-assembly process. Chapter 19 will scratch the surface for nature's self-assembly foundation as related to materials and manufacturing. This chapter will also begin to tell the story of nature's self-assembly for humans' learning processes.

We believe humans learn through a combined process of their genetics interacting with their environment. We further believe that this learning process begins to self-assemble knowledge and wisdom when people interact with positive outcomes, both recognized and rewarded. In summary, we plan to use our technology incubators as serendipity pools (see book 1) to prove that people who languish at the bottom of the wealth-inequality pyramid can form the foundation for great businesses created from vapor—solely from these self-assemblies of knowledge and wisdom. If we are successful, we plan to conduct many different clinical trials to study our results. We will then use the results of those clinical trials to determine if mental illness is the self-assembly wisdom process gone awry. For more information in this area, see the following:

> Like most aspects of human behavior and cognition, intelligence is a complex trait that is influenced by both genetic and environmental factors. Intelligence is challenging to study, in part because it can be defined and measured in different ways. Most definitions of intelligence include the ability to learn from experiences and adapt to changing environments. Elements of intelligence include the ability to reason, plan, solve problems, think abstractly, and understand complex ideas. Many studies rely on a measure of intelligence called the intelligence quotient (IQ).
>
> Researchers have conducted many studies to look for genes that influence intelligence. Many of these studies have focused on similarities and differences in IQ within families, particularly looking at adopted children and twins. Other studies have examined variations across the entire genomes of many people (an approach called genome-wide association studies or GWAS) to determine whether any specific areas of the genome are associated with IQ. Studies have not conclusively identified any genes that have major roles in differences in intelligence. It is likely that a large number of genes are involved, each of which makes only a small contribution to a person's intelligence. Other areas that contribute to intelligence, such as memory and verbal ability, involve additional genetic factors. Intelligence is also strongly influenced by the environment. During a child's development, factors that contribute to intelligence include their home environment and parenting, education and availability of learning resources, and healthcare and nutrition. A person's environment and genes influence each other,

and it can be challenging to tease apart the effects of the environment from those of genetics. For example, if a person's level of intelligence is similar to that of their parents, is that similarity due to genetic factors passed down from parent to child, to shared environmental factors, or (most likely) to a combination of both? It is clear that both environmental and genetic factors play a part in determining intelligence.[101]

Also read the article "Former Math Teacher Explains Why Some Students Are 'Good' at Math and Others Lag Behind" from *Science X*.[102]

It is no secret millions of people get lost in the system at some point during their lifetimes. Unfortunately, once they are lost, it is very difficult for them to recover. The explosion in homelessness is the most obvious example. One of our primary objectives for our clubhouse incubators will be to develop a national process that will identify how these people get lost and how we can help them recover.

16

Ending Crime and Prison Life

OUR NATION IS locked in a battle between a side that calls to defund the police and another that calls to fund them more. While this debate grinds on, crime and the number of innocent victims continue to climb. My first and second books discuss our recommendations for this area. In this chapter, we will focus on how the goal of 5 percent usable fresh water can eliminate both crime and prison life.

The land rushes set forth in chapter 10 can be used to empty all prisons, jails, detention centers, and other facilities—such as mental health and homeless encampments. Security is hardly a concern. Everyone will either be in the middle of a desert or on an ocean island. Where are they going to go? These migrations will give folks a fresh start in life. These migrations will also allow the criminal justice systems the opportunities to be much more aggressive in stopping crime in neighborhoods, making everyone relatively safe with new starts in life.

Ending Drug and Human-Trafficking Cartels

Another major benefit of digging the climate change lakes is that they will provide the geographic footprint to end where illegal drug, human trafficking, and other criminal activities take place. The economic opportunities to the people of Mexico will also help end the cartels.

17

The Wars on Religion, Spirituality, and the Hall of Souls: Secular False Prophecies

OUR NATION HAS swung in a secular direction. People are desperate to find meaning in their lives, but they are too busy just surviving to think about faith. Migration to the climate change lakes and climate change islands will provide those domestic migrants the opportunity to find more meaning and happiness in their lives. For more information, read the article "Social Media as We Know It Is Over" from *Yahoo Finance*.[103]

> Almost half of American workers say they "feel burned out at work" in a recent poll from Slack, the workplace messaging company. An overwhelming majority of companies say they see an increase in worker burnout. Employers, academics, and journalists are looking for the root causes of this phenomenon. So the root of millennial and Gen Z burnout isn't our economy or their bosses. It's their bad religion.[104]

When I attended my first Archway Publishing authors' conference for my first book, I was fortunate to meet a well-known gentleman who was both a retired US congressman and a pastor. We discussed my concentric villages that use prisons to build economic development strategies. He asked me, "Why not use churches at the center rather than prisons?"

I responded that churches were a great idea but explained that they would still leave the issue of providing physical security, because these people are still under the jurisdiction of the criminal justice system. He quickly understood. Then we began a lengthy discussion about using the same concentric circles strategy around churches for communities of people in the lowest-income areas but not under the criminal justice system.

Since that discussion, I have also had the opportunity to observe evolving new ministries that use contemporary technologies to build their churches—such as online video and communications that transcend millennia-long business models of worship, which are geographically focused and positioned.

Climate change lakes and islands could provide the opportunity for millions of people to obtain meaning and companionship in their lives. They could achieve this new meaning by combining traditional concepts of religion with secular populations, virtually coming together throughout the five desert and island areas to establish a new spiritual experience. This new spiritual experience would combine those believing in a higher power with those seeking spirituality through saving and being custodians for the planet—a sort of new Knights Templar organization that serves God while having a common purpose. Except these "knights" would protect the planet instead of Christian holy sites. They would protect and integrate pilgrims to the climate change lakes and islands instead of protecting Christian pilgrims in the Middle East and elsewhere.

18

Senior Housing and Circle of Life Retirement

THE AGING OF domestic and global populations is well known and previously discussed in my second book. Most older folks want to stay in their homes as they age—assuming they have a home. However, many aging populations never owned a home or have lost their homes due to rampant inflation. The homeless aging populations is reaching emergency levels for many communities. See the article "More Older Americans Become Homeless as Inflation Rises and Housing Costs Spike" from *NPR*.[105]

Not all "pilgrims" to the climate change lakes and climate change islands will have the immediate skills to form the leadership or green-energy workforce of climate change lakes and islands—especially those from prisons and homeless populations. But they will have the opportunity to contribute. They will just need a chance to perform and a job to fulfill that contributes to the national society. Establishing many multi-unit properties for aging Americans in climate change lakes and islands could add additional fabric to those new societies, relieve existing communities of housing burdens, and provide aging citizens with a new zest in the final years of their lives.

Unsurprisingly, prison populations are also aging. In many cases, prisons are already providing aging services.

> Our society is faced with the dilemma of aging prisoners, and some predict this will become one of the most important factors in managing the criminal justice system. Elderly inmates represent the fastest growing segment of federal and state prisons, a trend which is expected to continue. Hospice programs are growing in American correctional facilities, with access to health care professionals and efforts to provide a dignified death.[106]

19

Manufacture like Nature Manufactures— Understanding Self-Assembling

IN CHAPTER 8, we discussed the topic that it is only a matter of time before the world runs out of raw materials. This topic is closely related to the discussion of global warming. In chapter 15, we discussed self-assembly. Nature builds everything through a process of self-assembly. Understanding self-assembly in nature is the key to solving the problem of running out of raw materials. Many companies around the world are pioneering research and production in a vast number of different self-assembly areas and technologies.

Understanding Self-Assembly

Self-assembly of nanostructures is a process where atoms, molecules or nanoscale building blocks spontaneously organize into ordered structures or patterns with nanometer features without any human intervention. It is the most promising practical low-cost and high-throughput approach for nanofabrication.

The term "self-assembly" can be understood from its two components. The first component "self" implies "spontaneous and on its own," which suggests that it is a process that happens without human intervention or operation from outside of the system. The second component "assembly" indicates "forming or putting together," which suggests that the result is a structure built up by lower level building blocks or parts. Self-assembly of nanostructures refers to structures or patterns with nanometer features that form spontaneously from the basic building blocks such as atoms.[107]

A few examples of pioneering self-assembling efforts include self-assembling nanoparticles, self-assembling peptides, self-assembling polymers, self-assembling molecular crystals, and self-assembling monolayers. For more information, read the article "A New Quantum Component Made from Graphene" from *Science X*.[108]

Perhaps the most exciting area of research includes synthesizing biologics and combining those synthesized biologics with self-assembled materials. These combinations can essentially provide an unending array of new materials that can be synthetically manufactured. We only need to discover nature's secrets.

Think back to your middle school chemistry classroom, when you first saw the periodic table of the elements tacked on the wall. Now imagine a periodic table of new self-assembled elements on the wall. It would cover the entire wall, run out the door and into the hallway, cover every wall of every room and hallway in the entire school building, run into the gymnasium, and cover the entire gym with banners hanging from every rafter. Then it would run out of the gymnasium, into the town, and cover every building in the neighborhood.

Now imagine the school bell rings and you leave chemistry for home economics. Imagine the teacher hands everyone the recipe for a cake. You read the recipe: flour, eggs, baking soda, water, vanilla, and your favorite flavoring. If you were in a self-assembly recipe room, your old school computer would print six boxes of paper for each self-assembly recipe.

Imagine going to a next-generation shop class and pulling out a 3-D printer. You start printing your new 3-D biodegradable plastic. You want to "mix" it with a new high-strength steel ore that is nonrusting and indestructible. You put on a layer of steel then plastic and so on.

The number of new materials is exploding. I recently attended a conference where one of the speakers predicted that whichever country leads and owns the development of new materials will lead the world.

20

Addressing Strategic Atrophy and Reimagining Our Military-Industrial Complex and Civilian Relationships

IN MY FOURTH book, *Defeating the New Axis Powers*, we discussed what many in the military refer to as "strategic atrophy." If you have not read my fourth book, you should. You cannot solve global warming without understanding the geopolitics of climate change and global warming.

Strategic atrophy can be significantly addressed alongside the goal of 5 percent usable fresh water. Building the climate change islands could be especially useful. For example, building a chain of climate change islands around the Hawaiian Islands, Midway Island, Wake Island, and Guam could serve as bases for fleets of drone ships that could be used to patrol the Pacific Ocean. These fleets would be used to build the climate change islands and clean the oceans during peacetime. They could also quickly shift to military use to keep China in check if necessary. These fleets could number in the thousands—or even tens of thousands—and would be home bases for hundreds of thousands of drone swarm airplanes, submarines, and smart mines.

Reviving the US Shipbuilding Industry

The U.S. builds less than 10 vessels for oceangoing commerce in a typical year. China builds over a thousand such ships each year. The entire U.S.-registered fleet of oceangoing commercial ships numbers fewer than 200 vessels, out of a global total of 44,000. And despite trade flows to and from America exceeding a trillion dollars annually—the vast preponderance of which travel by sea—U.S.-registered ships carry barely 1% of that traffic. To make matters worse, the U.S. Navy has apparently lost its capacity to keep up with China in military shipbuilding. China now has the largest fleet of warships in the world, about 350, while America's Navy is struggling to get above 300. The Navy's request for ship construction funds next year envisions building only four combat vessels (out of eight total), a level of effort that if sustained would guarantee Chinese maritime dominance by 2030. U.S. sailors are still better trained and better equipped than their Chinese counterparts, but all the trends are in the wrong direction. It tells you a lot about the state of America's maritime sector that the largest exporter of containerized cargo to the U.S. is a shipping company owned outright by the Chinese government. The U.S. merchant marine today is so small that analysts question its ability to support military sealift requirements in a war. With only 180 or so oceangoing vessels in the U.S.-registered commercial fleet and less than 12,000 professional mariners—most whom would be tied up serving domestic routes at the onset of a war—the capacity of the private sector to supplement the government's aged collection of sealift vessels in an emergency is problematic at best. China's most immediate naval goal is to secure control of nearby seas; the smaller U.S. Navy needs to maintain a presence everywhere, from the North Atlantic to the Mediterranean Sea to the Persian Gulf to the Western Pacific.[109]

Review the following articles:

- "How Giant Ships Are Built"[110]
- "Beyond the Port: Shipbuilding in Jacksonville"[111]
- "China's Flying Submarine Drones the Future of Warfare"[112]

21

Paying Our Debts and Fixing
Our Financial Mess

IN MY FIRST and second books, we studied inequality economics. By inverting the wealth-inequality pyramid, we could eliminate the US national debt in approximately six years. The foundational strategy that we discussed was reindustrializing the US workforce to onshore manufacturing back from China. That opportunity still exists. In fact, it is already happening. As the US Federal Reserve continues to raise interest rates to combat inflation, many wonder how the labor market can remain relatively steady. I believe the answer is that US companies are already onshoring back from China.

If we combine the two initiatives from *Building the Selfless Economy* with our goal of 5 percent usable fresh water, we can easily pay for climate change and pay off the entire US national debt.

People can and should, prepare their own financial forecasts. You can begin with the data points included in chapter 12. You should also calculate your own estimates for the discounted net-values of these two initiatives. I have calculated a combined net present value between

$50 trillion and $100 trillion. For a conservative estimate, I assumed a combined value of $40 trillion and split it between the two initiatives—hence the $20 trillion each, which became the title of this book.

These values only include implementing the goal of 5 percent usable fresh water in North America. If the recommended additional countries were to adopt their own freshwater goals, the net present value would surely be in the hundreds of trillions of dollars. Even these estimates do not include the opportunity cost of saving the planet by building the climate change bridge, allowing net-zero carbon the centuries it will need. What is that worth? Everything.

The major policy assumptions I used in calculating my estimates included establishing a new US federal agency. This agency will manage building the infrastructure for the freshwater goal—including building the climate change lakes and climate change islands.

The agency should be authorized to provide seed financing up to $1 trillion over a ten-year period, which would be used to lend money and take equity positions in private companies to build the infrastructure. This $1 trillion could be financed directly by the US Federal Reserve. The authorization could be included in the enabling legislation. Unlike when the Federal Reserve buys general debt obligations, the issuing of this $1 trillion will not be inflationary. Markets will immediately understand the dramatic positive upside to the US economy.

The agency will manage the sale and/or lease of all desert properties. That money will be used to pay for the climate change lakes and islands. The agency will charge at least market rates for land sales, water rights, and other usage rights to maximize the cash flow from the initial infrastructure buildout. The agency will also recommend a *price list* of ongoing into perpetuity (e.g., fees, taxes, royalties, etc.) to Congress for them to enact into law. These ongoing revenues would be charged in addition to repaying the $1 trillion seed financing and initial cost of purchasing lands and water rights.

The agency will manage the planned land rushes as set forth in chapter 10. Priority will be given to people mired in the bottom 50 percent of the US wealth-inequality pyramid.

After the $1 trillion seed financing is repaid, the agency will continue to exist and operate with the mission of continuous management over the government's remaining properties and price list cash flows. The agency will be empowered to make recommendations to Congress to use ongoing revenues to make improvements to and maintain the climate change lakes and islands.

After the above allocations of cash flows are completed, residual cash flows would be sent to the Social Security Trust Fund to be used to fund Social Security and Medicare in the future.

The new cash flows generated from the private enterprise activities from the climate change lakes and islands will easily be able to pay off the national debt, fund Social Security, and fund Medicare. These payoffs will be greatly enabled by the significant reductions required for government transfer payments previously sent to the bottom of the wealth-inequality pyramid.

A summary of the nation's debts are listed below for reference purposes:

- US federal debt—$31.5 trillion
- Social Security unfunded liability—$23 trillion
- Medicare unfunded liability—$35 trillion
- student loan debt—$2 trillion[113]

> The gross national debt in America has hit new heights, surpassing $31 trillion, according to a recent U.S. treasury report. If you find that hard to wrap your head around, it basically boils down to more than $93,000 of debt for every person in the country, according to the Peter G. Peterson Foundation.[114]

Student Loans

Because of the politically charged nature of this issue, I have included a solution to the national problem of student loan debt. When I went to college, my wife and I paid for my undergraduate program and for both of our graduate programs. Much like many students today, we had to borrow money to finance our education. The difference is that there were no government loan programs at the time. Student loans were privately financed by banks.

> If someone wanted to destroy a generation's hope in their ability to get ahead, he could not have devised a better system than the federal government's income-based repayment plans. The federal government largely nationalized the student loan industry in 2010 via a piece of legislation related to Obamacare, the "Health Care and Education Reconciliation Act of 2010." The US government now holds 92 percent of all student loans—and the nation's total student debt has more than doubled, from $811 billion in April 2010 to $1.748 trillion in April 2022.[115]

> President Biden's plan to erase federal student loan debts for tens of millions of borrowers hit a legal wall Thursday, when a U.S. District Court judge in Texas called it unlawful and vacated the debt relief program. The federal government quickly appealed the decision, which came just weeks before student loan payments are set to resume in January. The program was already on hold while a federal appeals court in St. Louis considers a separate lawsuit by six states challenging it.[116]

Review the following articles:

- "Demise of Biden's Student Loan Handout Rocks Twitter: 'Its Only Purpose Was to Buy Votes'"[117]
- "Biden's Student Loan Cancellation Loses Again"[118]
- "Biden Administration Faces Tough Questions as Student Loan Plan Held Up in Court"[119]

- "Federal Appeals Court Blocks Biden Student Debt Relief Program Nationwide"[120]
- "Biden Administration to Make It Easier for Student Loan Borrowers to Discharge Debt in Bankruptcy"[121]
- "Student Loans: Advocates Cheer New Guidance for Debt Bankruptcy Discharges"[122]

Allowing bankruptcy for not repaying student loans but leaving government control over them goes against the original takeover structure in 2010. It is sort of like if you like your doctor, you can keep your doctor.

The Nation needs to help these student loan borrowers pay their loans. Yes, it was their decision to borrow the money, and any assistance is not fair to people who already paid their student loans back or never took out student loans. But the US government is complicit in getting these students in debt. What follows are my recommendations for how to fix the student loan crisis.

Start by setting a sunset date of December 31, 2025. After this date, the US government will no longer guarantee or make student loans. It will return the student loan industry back to the private sector. Normal bankruptcy laws would once again be in place for both lenders and borrowers of student loans.

The government should immediately freeze all outstanding student loans, stop interest accumulation on government loans, and negotiate a program for freezing the interest on private loans. Perhaps it could be paid by the college or university that the student attended.

To the student loan holder, the government should offer the option to continue making payments with no further interest or elect to have their employee portion of all future payroll taxes withheld to be allocated to pay off their student loan balances instead of being remitted to the Social Security Trust Fund. The IRS and Social Security Administration could easily work out these transfers, making it seamless to the student loan holder.

After their student loans are entirely paid off, the loan holder's future employee portion of their payroll taxes would revert back to the Social Security Trust Fund. The student would also have the option of withholding an additional amount to pay back the portion of their payroll taxes that went to paying off their student loans. The Social Security Administration would maintain the necessary records online. If the student loan borrower reaches retirement and has not paid back all their debt, then their Social Security benefits would be reduced accordingly.

Any student loan borrower who has elected this program will not be eligible for inclusion in the land rushes set forth in chapter 10.

22

ESG Investing By Prophecy

WE HAD A detailed discussion on ESG in my second book. I have included a follow-up chapter here to begin injecting the concept of prophecy into the ESG investing process. Congress and the courts will soon sort out what is legal from a fiduciary perspective. This chapter is devoted to looking at ESG investing solely through the lens of benchmarking the goal of 5 percent usable fresh water against net-zero carbon.

Net-zero carbon and 5 percent usable fresh water are not mutually exclusive strategies. On the contrary, they are very much synergistic when combined into a total and permanent strategy. But the key differences are that the freshwater goal is a short-term strategy designed for making money and directly targets rising ocean coastlines, desertification, ocean pollution, biodiversity loss, freshwater depletion, and inflation. Net-zero carbon is an admitted long-term strategy singularly designed to throw a lot of money at lowering carbon emissions in the hope that it will solve all such issues.

The world is waking up to the fact the climate-policy goal of achieving "net-zero" CO_2 emissions brings crippling economic pain. As fossil-fuel prices climb, activists believe people will shift painlessly to renewable energy sources. But they've made a major miscalculation: Renewables are far from ready to power the world.

McKinsey estimates getting to net-zero will cost Europe 5.3% of its GDP in low-emission assets every year, or more than $200 billion annually just for Germany. That's more than it spends annually on education and police, courts and prisons combined. The United States has gone all-in on its own net-zero ambition with the most expensive climate-change policy in its history. With the Inflation Reduction Act, the Biden administration plans to spend $369 billion promoting low-carbon energy and electric vehicles. This vast expenditure will have a negligible impact on climate change, reducing the global temperature rise unmeasurably, possibly as low as 0.0009°F. [123]

"The actual environmental benefits of 'green' energy are few and far between, if there are any at all. Yet its economic and national security impact is immeasurably negative," the experts wrote in the letter. "Compromising American energy security for the sake of climate alarmism is more than a misstep, it is a catastrophic error – just look at Europe." [124]

Review the article "ESG and the 'Long-Run Interests' Dodge" from the *Wall Street Journal*. [125]

23

Case Studies: Learning the Two $20 Trillion Opportunities

THE CASE STUDIES presented in this chapter will help you learn, understand, and implement the two $20 trillion opportunities.

Case Study 1: Goal of 5 Percent Usable Fresh Water

Topic Introduction

Explain your understanding of the goal of 5 percent usable fresh water.

Reader's Topic Analysis

Reader's Conclusions and Recommendations

Case Study 2: Goal of 5 Percent Usable Fresh Water

Topic Introduction

Do you agree with the author's recommendation that the freshwater goal should be the top climate change goal? Why or why not?

Reader's Topic Analysis

Reader's Conclusions and Recommendations

Case Study 3: Goal of 5 Percent Usable Fresh Water

Topic Introduction

Do you agree with the author that the hurdle test for the thirty-year mortgage is a fair test to benchmark global warming strategies against? Why or why not?

Reader's Topic Analysis

Reader's Conclusions and Recommendations

Case Study 4: Goal of 5 Percent Usable Fresh Water

Topic Introduction

Do you believe the freshwater goal is a politically viable and consensus-building strategy? Why or why not?

Reader's Topic Analysis

Reader's Conclusions and Recommendations

Case Study 5: Goal of 5 Percent Usable Fresh Water

Topic Introduction

Do you agree with the author that the freshwater goal is the best path forward for helping developing countries' global warming transition? Why or why not?

Reader's Topic Analysis

Reader's Conclusions and Recommendations

Case Study 6: Goal of 5 Percent Usable Fresh Water

Topic Introduction

Explain the author's position on the idea that the freshwater goal is a direct strategy that goes on offense, but net-zero carbon is an indirect strategy that is purely defensive. Do you agree with the author? Why or why not?

Reader's Topic Analysis

Reader's Conclusions and Recommendations

Case Study 7: Climate Change Lakes and Islands

Topic Introduction

Explain the author's strategy for climate change lakes and islands. Do you believe this is a viable strategy? Why or why not?

Reader's Topic Analysis

Reader's Conclusions and Recommendations

Case Study 8: Ocean Water Transfer Credits

Topic Introduction

Explain the concept of ocean water transfer credits and how you believe they are envisioned to work.

Reader's Topic Analysis

Reader's Conclusions and Recommendations

Case Study 9: Ocean Water Transfer Credits

Topic Introduction

Compare and contrast ocean water transfer credits against carbon transfer credits and carbon offsets. Include your opinion of their relative values.

Reader's Topic Analysis

Reader's Conclusions and Recommendations

Case Study 10: Super-Emitters

Topic Introduction
Explain super-emitters.

Reader's Topic Analysis

Reader's Conclusions and Recommendations

Case Study 11: Land Rushes for Climate
Change Lakes and Islands

Topic Introduction
Do you agree with the author's strategy and tactics for land rushes? Why or why not?

Reader's Topic Analysis

Reader's Conclusions and Recommendations

Case Study 12: Positives from Global Warming

Topic Introduction
Do you believe there are positives from global warming that should be retained if possible? If yes, what are they? If no, why not?

Reader's Topic Analysis

Reader's Conclusions and Recommendations

Case Study 13: Paying for Climate Change

Topic Introduction
Explain the strengths and weaknesses of the author's recommendations for paying for climate change.

Reader's Topic Analysis

Reader's Conclusions and Recommendations

Case Study 14: Paying for Climate Change

Topic Introduction
List and explain your recommendations for how best to pay for climate change.

Reader's Topic Analysis

Reader's Conclusions and Recommendations

Case Study 15: The Selfless Economy

Topic Introduction
Explain your understanding of the selfless economy.

Reader's Topic Analysis

Reader's Conclusions and Recommendations

Case Study 16: Community Leadership Layering

Topic Introduction
Explain your understanding of community leadership layering.

Reader's Topic Analysis

Reader's Conclusions and Recommendations

Case Study 17: Clubhouse Incubators

Topic Introduction
Explain your understanding of clubhouse incubators.

Reader's Topic Analysis

Reader's Conclusions and Recommendations

Case Study 18: Ending Crime and Prison Life

Topic Introduction
Do you agree with the author that both crime and prison life can be stopped by building climate change lakes and islands? Why or why not?

Reader's Topic Analysis

Reader's Conclusions and Recommendations

Case Study 19: Self-Assembling in Nature

Topic Introduction
Explain your understanding of self-assembling technologies.

Reader's Topic Analysis

Reader's Conclusions and Recommendations

Case Study 20: Military Strategic Atrophy

Topic Introduction
Explain your understanding of military strategic atrophy.

Reader's Topic Analysis

Reader's Conclusions and Recommendations

Case Study 21: Paying Our Debts

Topic Introduction

Prepare an analysis of "Paying Our Debts and Fixing Our Financial Mess" from chapter 21.

Reader's Topic Analysis

Reader's Conclusions and Recommendations

NOTES

Introduction

- *The Two $20 Trillion Opportunities* is the third and final part of a three-part series

Chapter 1

- Goal of 5 percent usable fresh water
- Providing hope for a great future
- Immediate economic payback—clears the thirty-year-mortgage test hurdle
- Politically viable and consensus-enabling strategy
- Growing capitulation that net-zero carbon and Paris Agreement have no chance of success

Chapter 2

- Climate change lakes in North America
- A high level diagram of the five North American deserts and geographics for the goal of 5percent usable fresh water
- Climate change islands in North America

Chapter 3

- Industrial chillers in fighting global warming and climate change

Chapter 4

- Rebuilding mountain snowcaps and mountain glaciers

Chapter 5

- Brine mountains
- Twenty-first-century monasteries

Chapter 6

- Climate change lakes and islands outside North America

Chapter 7

- Ocean water transfer credits

Chapter 8

- Partnering with seafloor mining

Chapter 9

- NASA super-emitter research

Chapter 10

- Land Rushes of 1889, 2050, 2075, and 2100

Preview

The Leadership Broadcasting Company

THE DECISION-MAKING NETWORK

The Leadership Broadcasting Company launches the JM Prophecies Corporation media company.

Channel 1

Channel 1 –Understanding and Solving Climate Change will consist entirely of filmed documentaries and town hall meetings. Some of these documentaries and meetings will be televised live, and some will be recorded and replayed later. All documentaries and meetings will be filmed at onsite locations. We are still planning the playlist, which will likely continue to change over time—dependent upon real time activities and results. However, an EST Monday-through-Sunday sample programming list for *Channel 1* is provided in the following.

➢ 6:00am–7:00am: Building Climate Change Islands and Extending the Florida Everglades in the Caribbean, Florida Keys, and Guantanamo Bay

➢ 7:00am–8:00am: Slowing and Stopping Rising Ocean Coastlines on the US Atlantic Coast and Gulf of Mexico

➢ 8:00am–9:00am: Rebuilding Freshwater Supplies in the Midwest, Mississippi River Valley, and Missouri River Valley

➢ 9:00am–10:00am: Building Climate Change Lakes in the US (morning show)

➢ 10:00am–11:00am: Building Climate Change Lakes in Mexico (9:00am Mexico City local time)

➢ 11:00am–12:00pm: Saving the Great Salt Lake

➢ 12:00pm–1:00pm: Rebuilding Freshwater Supplies in the Colorado River Basin and the Broader Southwest

➢ 1:00pm–2:00pm: Rebuilding US Mountain Snowcaps and Glaciers

➢ 2:00pm–3:00pm: Building Climate Change Lakes in the US (afternoon show)

➢ 3:00pm–4:00pm: Building Desalination Plants, Energy Plants, and Other Infrastructure Surrounding the North American Climate Change Lakes

➤ 4:00pm–5:00pm: Economic Development Around the North American Climate Change Lakes Shorelines

➤ 5:00pm–6:00pm: Economic Development Around the North American Climate Change Lakes Desalinated Freshwater Supplies

➤ 6:00pm–7:00pm: Hosting Federal, State, and Local Authorities' Forums, Meetings, and Planning Discussions

➤ 7:00pm–8:00pm: LBC Town Hall Meetings First Hour

➤ 8:00pm–9:00pm: LBC Town Hall Meetings Second Hour

➤ 9:00pm–10:00pm: LBC Town Hall Meetings Third Hour

➤ 10:00pm–11:00pm: Building Climate Change Lakes in the US (night show)

➤ 11:00pm–12:00am: Building Climate Change Lakes and Climate Change Islands in South America (1:00am Rio de Janeiro local time)

➤ 12:00am–1:00am: Building Climate Change Islands in Hawaii, Alaska, Midway Island, Wake Island, and Guam (7:00pm Honolulu local time)

➤ 1:00am–2:00am: LBC Town Hall Meetings in Africa (7:00am Abuja, Nigeria, local time)

> 2:00am–3:00am: Building Climate Change Lakes in the Middle East Deserts (10:00am Bagdad local time, 10:00am Riyadh local time, and 9:00am Jerusalem local time)

> 3:00am–4:00am: Building Climate Change Lakes in the Sahara Desert and the Mediterranean Sea (10:00am Cairo local time, 9:00am Morocco local time, 9:00am Rome local time, and 9:00am Marseille local time)

> 4:00am–5:00am: Building Climate Change Lakes and Climate Change Islands in Australia (8:00pm Sydney local time)

> 5:00am–6:00am: LBC Town Hall Meetings in Europe (11:00am Warsaw local time, 11:00am Berlin local time, 11:00am Paris local time, and 10:00am London local time)

Channel 2

Channel 2 –Stopping Biodiversity Loss will consist entirely of filmed documentaries and town hall meetings. Some of these documentaries and meetings will be televised live, and some will be recorded and replayed later. All documentaries and meetings will be filmed at onsite locations. We are still planning the playlist.

Channel 3

Channel 3 –Defeating the New Axis Powers will consist entirely of filmed documentaries and town hall meetings. Some of these documentaries and meetings will be televised live, and some will be recorded and replayed later. All documentaries and meetings will be filmed at onsite locations. We are still planning the playlist.

Channel 4

Channel 4 –The Decision Making Network. We are still planning the playlist and strategies.

Channel 5

Channel 5 –Integrating Western Hemisphere Economies. We are still planning the playlist and strategies.

Preview

Integrating the Economies of the Western Hemisphere

Integrating the Economies of the Western Hemisphere begins to build the serendipity pools and strategies for how we can finally integrate the economies of the Western Hemisphere for the advancement of all countries in that hemisphere.

Preview

Crossing Waldo Road

BIRTHPLACE OF THE SELFLESS ECONOMY

Crossing Waldo Road lays out the birthplace of the selfless economy.

Preview

The Western Hemisphere Stock Exchange

LAUNCHING A NEW KIND OF STOCK EXCHANGE

The Western Hemisphere Stock Exchange will provide a new financing pathway for *Building the Selfless Economy*.

Preview

Building the Selfless Economy

THE ELITES NO LONGER HAVE THE RIGHT STUFF

PERHAPS THEY NEVER DID

REFERENCES

1   David Nield, *Science Alert*, October 29, 2022, https://www.sciencealert.com/almost-half-of-earths-vital-signs-are-now-code-red-scientists-warn.

2   Mathis Wackernagel, *GEF*, November 14, 2017, https://www.thegef.org/news/humanity-uses-70-more-global-commons-earth-can-regenerate.

3   Stockholm Resilience Center, accessed October 31, 2022, https://www.stockholmresilience.org/research/planetary-boundaries/the-nine-planetary-boundaries.html.

4   Agence France-Presse, *South China Morning Post*, November 7, 2022, https://www.scmp.com/economy/china-economy/article/3191840/china-population-urbanisation-offers-huge-source-untapped?module=perpetual_scroll_1&pgtype=article&campaign=3191840.

5   Sharon Pruitt-Young, *NPR*, September 4, 2021, https://www.npr.org/2021/09/14/1037023551/climate-change-children-young-adults-anxious-worried-study.

6   Marie Haaland, *SWNS*, September 6, 2021, https://swnsdigital.com/us/2020/04/majority-of-young-american-adults-say-climate-change-influences-their-decision-to-have-children/.

7   Sarah Simon, *Very well health*, April 19, 2021, https://www.verywellhealth.com/gen-z-climate-change-anxiety-survey-5179490.

8   "Changing Weather Could Put Insurance Firms Out of Business," *The Economist*, September 19, 2019, https://www.economist.com/finance-and-economics/2019/09/19/changing-weather-could-put-insurance-firms-out-of-business?utm_medium=cpc.adword.pd&utm_source=google&ppccampaignID=17210591673&ppcadID=&utm_campaign=a.22brand_pmax-&utm_content=conversion.direct-response.anonymous&gclid=EAIaIQobC

hMI7ZCj6b2f-wIVmBXUAR2CJAuQEAMYASAAEgLOvvD_BwE&gcl-src=aw.ds.

9	Diana Olick, "Mortgage Market Is Unprepared for Climate Risk, Says Industry Report," *CNBC*, September 23, 2021, https://www.cnbc.com/2021/09/23/mortgage-market-is-unprepared-for-climate-risk-says-industry-report.html.

10	Christopher Flavelle, "Rising Seas Threaten an American Institution: The 30-Year Mortgage," *New York Times*, June 19, 2020, https://www.nytimes.com/2020/06/19/climate/climate-seas-30-year-mortgage.html.

11	Jennifer Sor, *Markets Insider*, November 15, 2022, https://markets.businessinsider.com/news/stocks/recession-fed-tightening-rate-hike-pivot-pause-inflation-falling-citi-2022-11.

12	Christopher Rugaber, *ABC News*, November 17, 2022, https://abcnews.go.com/Business/wireStory/fed-official-suggests-substantial-rate-hikes-needed-93479550.

13	Carmen Reinicke, *CNBC*, November 17, 2022, https://www.cnbc.com/2022/11/17/starwoods-sternlicht-says-what-the-fed-is-doing-to-economy-is-suicide.html.

14	Irina Slav, *Oil Price*, November 18, 2022. https://oilprice.com/Energy/Heating-Oil/New-Englanders-Are-Fed-Up-With-High-Energy-Prices.html.

15	Thomas Catenacci, *Fox Business*, November 21, 2022. https://www.foxbusiness.com/politics/energy-group-issues-roadmap-house-republicans-boost-us-energy-security.

16	Lois Parshley, *New Scientist*, November 1, 2022. https://www.newscientist.com/article/2344912-the-us-megadrought-wont-just-end-it-will-change-the-land-forever/.

17	James Dinneen, *New Scientist*, October 28, 2022, https://www.newscientist.com/article/2344377-what-is-causing-the-megadroughts-in-north-and-south-america/.

18	Chelsea Harvey, *Scientific American*, February 15, 2022, https://www.scientificamerican.com/article/western-megadrought-is-the-worst-in-1-200-years/.

19	Mark Fischetti, *Scientific American*, February 12, 2015, https://www.scientificamerican.com/article/u-s-droughts-will-be-the-worst-in-1-000-years1/.

20	Robyn White, *Newsweek*, November 15, 2022, https://www.newsweek.com/mississippi-river-drying-1759697.

21	James Dinneen, *New Scientist*, November 17, 2022, https://www.newscientist.com/article/2347393-us-megadrought-could-upend-life-as-we-know-it-just-look-to-history/.

22	Anna Novoselov, "Megadrought in Southwestern North America Is Region's Driest in At Least 1,200 Years," *UCLA Newsroom*, February 14, 2022, https://newsroom.ucla.edu/releases/megadrought-southwestern-north-america.

23 Julia Jacobo and Daniel Manzo, "Megadrought out West Expected to Intensify, Expand East: NOAA," *ABC News*, April 12, 2022, https://abcnews. go.com/US/megadrought-west-expected-intensify-expand-east-noaa/story?id=84221152.

24 Bob Henson, "Climate Change Is Stoking What May Be a Long-Term Megadrought in Western U.S.," *The Weather Channel*, April 16, 2020, https:// weather.com/news/climate/news/2020-04-16-climate-change-stoking-long-term-megadrought-western-us?cm_ven=PS_GGL_DSA_09162019_1&par=MK_GGL&tpcc=mktg-search-Google-acquisition&gclid=EAIaIQobChMIpbCM3dCR-wIVJilMCh23SQ4IEAMYASAAEgLR1fD_BwE.

25 Felicity Bradstock, "The Global Water Crisis Could Crush the Energy Industry," *Oil Price*, September 23, 2022, https://oilprice.com/Energy/Energy-General/The-Global-Water-Crisis-Could-Crush-The-Energy-Industry.html.

26 Diana Olick, "Microsoft, Meta and Others Face Rising Drought Risk to Their Data Centers," *CNBC*, November 15, 2022, https://www.cnbc.com/2022/11/15/microsoft-meta-others-face-rising-drought-risk-to-their-data-centers.html.

27 Xander Huggins, "Ripple Effect: As Global Freshwater Basins Dry Up, the Threat to Ecosystems and Communities Grows," *Science X*, November 3, 2022, https://phys.org/news/2022-11-ripple-effect-global-freshwater-basins.html.

28 Saul Elbein and Sharon Udasin, November 10, 2022, https://thehill.com/policy/equilibrium-sustainability/3730176-equilibrium-sustainability-a-rainy-future-for-the-desert-southwest/.

29 The Associated Press, "Greenhouse Gases Reach a New Record as Nations Fall Behind on Climate Pledges," *NPR*, October 26, 2022, https://www.npr.org/2022/10/26/1131671933/greenhouse-gases-record-climate-pledges-un.

30 Catherine Clifford, "Bill Gates' Climate-Investment Firm Will Put More Money into Adapting to Climate Change," *CNBC*, October 25, 2022, https://www.cnbc.com/2022/10/25/bill-gates-climate-tech-investing-company-bev-moving-into-adaptation.html.

31 Al Jazeera, "World on Highway to Climate Hell, UN Chief Guterres Tells COP27," November 7, 2022, https://www.aljazeera.com/news/2022/11/7/world-on-highway-to-climate-hell-un-chief-guterres-tells-cop27.

32 Doug Cunningham, "Greenland Ice Sheet Shows Extensive Inland Thinning, Faster Sea Level Rise." *AccuWeather*, November 11, 2022, https://www.accuweather.com/en/climate/report-greenland-ice-sheet-shows-extensive-inland-thinning-faster-sea-level-rise/1277157.

33 *Oil Price*, "The U.S. Might Need to Increase Electricity Generation by 480%," November 11, 2022, https://oilprice.com/Energy/Energy-General/The-US-Might-Need-To-Increase-Electricity-Generation-By-480.html.

34 Jeff Tollefson, "Carbon Emissions Hit New High: Warning from COP27," *Nature*, November 11, 2022, https://www.nature.com/articles/d41586-022-03657-w.

35 Michael Freilich, "NASA Study: Rising Sea Level Could Exceed Estimates for U.S. Coasts," *NASA*, November 15, 2022, https://www.nasa.gov/feature/jpl/nasa-study-rising-sea-level-could-exceed-estimates-for-us-coasts.

36 Chantal Da Silva, *NBC News*, October 26, 2022, https://www.nbcnews.com/news/world/world-emissions-paris-climate-targets-un-report-rcna54044.

37 Carter Dillard, *The Hill*, April 23, 2022, https://thehill.com/opinion/energy-environment/3460944-the-paris-agreement-is-failing-we-need-a-new-approach/.

38 CDP, September 6, 2022, https://www.cdp.net/en/articles/investor/g7-firms-failing-paris-agreement.

39 Ivana Kottasova, *CNN*, September 16, 2021, https://www.cnn.com/2021/09/15/world/climate-pledges-insufficient-cat-intl/index.html.

40 Nicolas Loris, *The Heritage Foundation*, February 25, 2021. https://www.heritage.org/energy-economics/report/paris-climate-agreement-instead-regulations-and-mandates-embrace-markets?gclid=EAIaIQobChMImP6jr96R-wIV0gN9Ch3YgQgPEAMYASAAEgL4IPD_BwE.

41 Anmar Frangoul, *CNBC*, November 17, 2022, https://www.cnbc.com/2022/11/17/energy-transition-will-fail-unless-wind-power-fixes-problems-ceo.html.

42 Peter Prengaman, *AP News*, November 17, 2022. https://apnews.com/article/g-20-summit-climate-and-environment-d8bd7530e445c0e7987c69677881a88d

43 Lora Kolodny and Michael Wayland, *CNBC*, November 15, 2022, https://www.cnbc.com/2022/11/15/consumer-reports-new-technologies-make-evs-less-reliable.html.

44 Michael Copley, November 9, 2022, https://www.npr.org/2022/11/09/1134865038/investors-have-trillions-to-fight-climate-change-developing-nations-get-little-o.

45 *Nature*, "COP27: Rich Countries Must Stop Stalling Talks on Climate Loss and Damage Compensation," November 8, 2022, https://www.nature.com/articles/d41586-022-03596-6.

46 Simplice Nouala, Al Jazeera, November 10, 2022, https://www.aljazeera.com/opinions/2022/11/10/livestock-is-a-form-of-climate-justice-in-the-global-south.

47 *Euronews*, November 12, 2022, https://www.euronews.com/2022/11/12/watc
h-protesters-call-for-compensation-from-wealthy-nations-at-cop27.

48 Alex Kimani, *Oil Price*, November 12, 2022, https://oilprice.com/Energy/
Crude-Oil/Exxon-Mobil-Makes-First-Oil-Discovery-In-Angola-In-20-Years.
html.

49 Thomas Catenacci, *Fox News*, November 15, 2022, https://www.foxnews.
com/politics/left-wing-green-agenda-backed-john-kerry-disaster-developing-
world-experts-say.

50 Caitlin McFall, *Fox News*, November 15, 2022, https://www.foxnews.com/
politics/biden-announces-20b-move-indonesia-away-coal.

51 Michael Copley, *NPR*, November 16, 2022, https://www.npr.
org/2022/11/16/1136817427/low-income-countries-want-more-money-f
or-climate-damage-theyre-unlikely-to-get-i.

52 Dan Hannan, *Washington Examiner*, November 21, 2022, https://www.
washingtonexaminer.com/opinion/demands-for-climate-reparations-are
-laughable.

53 Leila Sackur, "Should Rich Countries Pay Climate 'Reparations'? Why the
Debate Is on the COP27 Agenda," *NBC News*, November 15, 2022, https://
www.nbcnews.com/news/world/climate-reparations-cop27-what-it-means-
rcna49105.

54 Zack Budryk, "UN Climate Summit Releases Draft of Long-Sought 'Loss
and Damage' Agreement," The Hill, November 14, 2022, https://thehill.
com/policy/energy-environment/3735171-un-climate-summit-releases-draft-
of-long-sought-loss-and-damage-agreement/.

55 Matthew Dalton, Stacy Meichtry, and Summer Said, "COP27 Agrees on
Loss and Damage Fund for Vulnerable Countries, Officials Say," *Wall
Street Journal*, November 19, 2022, https://www.wsj.com/articles/cop2
7-agrees-on-loss-and-damage-fund-for-vulnerable-countries-officials-say-
11668866219?mod=mhp.

56 Sam Meredith, "Historic Deal for Poorer Nations as COP Climate Summit Agrees to 'Loss and Damage' Fund," *CNBC*, updated November 21,
2022, https://www.cnbc.com/2022/11/20/cop27-new-global-climate-dea
l-struck-at-conference-in-egypt.html.

57 Zack Colman and Karl Mathiesen. "Nations Reach Preliminary Deal on
Payments as Climate Talks Grind through Overtime," *Politico*, November 19,
2022, https://www.politico.com/news/2022/11/19/nations-close-to-agreemen
t-on-payments-as-climate-talks-near-end-00069589.

58 *Climate Action Network International*, "Landmark Decision at Cop27 to Set
Up Loss and Damage Fund," November 20, 2022, https://climatenetwork.
org/2022/11/20/landmark-decision-at-cop27-to-set-up-loss-and-damage-fund/.

59 Luis Chaparro, "The Sinaloa Cartel Is Controlling Water in Drought-Stricken Mexico," *Vice World News*, September 20, 2022, https://www.vice.com/en/article/4ax479/mexico-sinaloa-cartel-water.

60 Ben Adler, November 14, 2022, https://news.yahoo.com/mexico-releases-ambitious-renewable-energy-targets-to-fight-climate-change-222911242.html.

61 Lucy Sherriff, November 7, 2022, https://finance.yahoo.com/news/seaweed-superfood-revolution-could-end-180000023.html.

62 November 18, 2022, https://komonews.com/news/local/fish-farms-washington-state-dnr-department-of-natural-resources-commercial-finfish-net-pen-aquaculture-hillary-franz-commissioner-public-lands-salish-bainbridge-tribe-suquamish.

63 Stanford University, "Dams Could Play a Big Role in Feeding the World More Sustainably, Researchers Find," *Science X*, November 14, 2022, https://phys.org/news/2022-11-play-big-role-world-sustainably.html.

64 *France 24*, September 28, 2022, https://www.france24.com/en/live-news/20220928-half-world-s-birds-in-decline-species-moving-ever-faster-to-extinction.

65 Andrew Van Dam, *Washington Post*, September 23, 2022, https://www.washingtonpost.com/business/2022/09/23/american-territories-population-loss/.

66 Emily C. Nunez, *Maryland Today*, November 7, 2022, https://today.umd.edu/study-warns-of-climate-changes-looming-devastation-of-insect-species.

67 Juli Berwald, *Nautilus*, November 11, 2022, https://nautil.us/coral-restoration-goes-big-246102/.

68 SINTEF, "Fjord Ice Can Have a Great Impact on Local Communities," *Science X*, November 9, 2022, https://phys.org/news/2022-11-fjord-ice-great-impact-local.html.

69 Tereza Pultarova, "Sea Levels Might Rise Much Faster Than Thought, Data from Greenland Suggest," *Space.com*, November 9, 2022, https://www.space.com/greenland-ice-melting-satellite-data-climate-change.

70 Kris Maher and Christine Mai-Duc, November 11, 2022, A3.

71 Leslie Kaufman and Will Wade, November 8, 2022, https://finance.yahoo.com/news/tiny-insurance-company-standing-between-100013813.html.

72 Bradford Betz, November 6, 2022, https://www.foxnews.com/politics/cop27-delegates-weigh-climate-compensation-poor-nations-impacted-global-warming; Matthew Smith, November 5, 2022, https://oilprice.com/Energy/Crude-Oil/Guyanas-Offshore-Drilling-Bonanza-Is-Just-Getting-Started.html.

73 Will Kenton, "Carbon Credits and How They Can Offset Your Carbon Footprint," *Investopedia*, August 19, 2022. https://www.investopedia.com/terms/c/carbon_credit.asp#:~:text=Carbon%20credits%2C%20also%20known%20as,%2Dand%2Dtrade%22%20program.

74   Kyle Peterdy, "Carbon Credits," *Corporate Finance Institute*, August 19, 2022, https://corporatefinanceinstitute.com/resources/esg/carbon-credit/.

75   Christopher Blaufelder, Cindy Levy, Peter Mannion, and Dickon Pinner, "A Blueprint for Scaling Voluntary Carbon Markets to Meet the Climate Challenge," *McKinsey Sustainability*, January 29, 2021, https://www.mckinsey.com/capabilities/sustainability/our-insights/a-blueprint-for-scaling-voluntary-carbon-markets-to-meet-the-climate-challenge.

76   Marcel Honore, October 31, 2022, https://www.civilbeat.org/2022/10/north-shore-group-confronts-growing-threats-of-erosion-sea-level-rise/.

77   Danica Coto, "Search for Minerals Increases Interest in Deep-Sea Mining," *Science & Technology*, November 10, 2022, https://learningenglish.voanews.com/a/search-for-minerals-increases-interest-in-deep-sea-mining/6819939.html.

78   Eyck Freymann, "The Ocean Edge," *The Wire China*, November 6, 2022, https://www.thewirechina.com/2022/11/06/china-seabed-mining/.

79   Jocelyn Trainer, "The Geopolitics of Deep-Sea Mining and Green Technologies," *United States Institute of Peace*, November 3, 2022, https://www.usip.org/publications/2022/11/geopolitics-deep-sea-mining-and-green-technologies.

80   "Methane 'Super-Emitters' Mapped by NASA's New Earth Space Mission," NASA, October 25, 20222, https://www.nasa.gov/feature/jpl/methane-super-emitters-mapped-by-nasa-s-new-earth-space-mission.

81   Julianne Geiger, November 9, 2022, https://oilprice.com/Latest-Energy-News/World-News/US-And-EU-To-Crack-Down-On-Fossil-Fuel-Sectors-Methane-Emissions.html.

82   Tsvetana Paraskova, "UN Launches Satellite System to Track Methane Emissions," *Oil Price*, November 11, 2022, https://oilprice.com/Latest-Energy-News/World-News/UN-Launches-Satellite-System-To-Track-Methane-Emissions.html.

83   Geoffrey Migiro, "Which Deserts Are in North America?" *World Atlas*, October 31, 2018, https://www.worldatlas.com/articles/which-deserts-are-in-north-america.html.

84   Brian Philpot, *The Hill*, November 1, 2022, https://thehill.com/opinion/finance/3714195-looming-food-crisis-we-need-to-keep-farmland-in-the-hands-of-farmers/.

85   Alex Lubben, *Vice News*, October 13, 2022, https://www.vice.com/en/article/k7bp5e/houston-mobile-home-buyout-flood-risks.

86   Konrad Putzier, *Wall Street Journal*, September 25, 2022, https://www.wsj.com/articles/the-u-s-is-running-short-of-land-for-housing-11664125841.

87   Robert Huang and Matthew Kahn, "Get Ready for the Great American Land Rush," *Business Insider*, November 15, 2022, https://www.busines-

sinsider.com/great-american-land-rush-land-housing-wind-power-solar-p
anels-2022-11.

88 Moira Donovan, November 3, 2022, https://hakaimagazine.com/fea-
tures/greenlands-melting-ice-sheet-brings-an-unexpected-flow-of-wealth-
potential/.

89 "Mission 2016: The Future of Strategic Natural Resources," MIT, accessed
November 6, 2022, https://web.mit.edu/12.000/www/m2016/finalwebsite/
solutions/newmines.html.

90 Eric Markowitz, "What If Boston Shipped All Its Snow To Water-Starved
California?", Vocativ, February 10, 2015, https://www.vocativ.com/culture/
science/boston-blizzard-california-drought/index.html.

91 Ben Winslow, "How Much It Might Cost to Build a Pipeline to Fill the
Great Salt Lake," *Fox 13*, October 13, 2022, https://www.fox13now.com/
news/local-news/how-much-it-might-cost-to-build-a-pipeline-to-fill-the-great
-salt-lake.

92 Al Jazeera, "What the Latest IPCC Science Says about Climate Change," November 6, 2022, https://www.aljazeera.com/news/2022/11/6/what-the-lates
t-ipcc-science-says-about-climate-change.

93 Grace O'Donnell, "Net Zero Could Lead to 'the Largest Redeployment
of Capital in History,'" *Yahoo Finance*, November 1, 2022, https://finance.
yahoo.com/news/net-zero-largest-redeployment-of-capital-in-history-bny-mel-
lon-171509117.html.

94 Trey Williams, November 9, 2022, https://fortune.com/2022/11/09/america
n-middle-class-jobs-disappearing/; November 15, 2022, https://thefishsite.
com/articles/global-aquaculture-deemed-to-be-in-decline.

95 Olivia Weeks, "The 40-Year Robbing of Rural America," *In These Times*,
October 3, 2022, https://inthesetimes.com/article/financial-capital-sacrific
e-zones-robbing-rural-america.

96 University of California—Santa Cruz, "Scientists Show Transmission of
Epigenetic Memory across Multiple Generations," SciTech Daily, October 4,
2022, https://scitechdaily.com/scientists-show-transmission-of-epigenetic-m
emory-across-multiple-generations/.

97 Mike Battista, "22 Genes Have Been Linked to Intelligence, but DNA Is
Not Your Destiny," *Creyos*, accessed November 11, 2022, https://creyos.com/
resources/articles/22-genes-linked-to-intelligence.

98 Allison Gatlin November 16, 2022, https://www.investors.com/news/technol-
ogy/biotech-stocks-embrace-neuroscience-renaissance-with-biogen-amylyx-a
t-the-helm/.

99 Allana Akhtar, October 7, 2022, https://www.insider.com/psychiatric-nurs
e-said-injury-violence-on-the-job-worsened-covid-2022-9.

100 Pedro Conceicao, "Human Development in an Age of Uncertainty," *Brookings*, November 4, 2022, https://www.brookings.edu/blog/future-development/2022/11/04/human-development-in-an-age-of-uncertainty/.

101 "Is Intelligence Determined by Genetics?" Medline Plus, accessed November 11, 2022, https://medlineplus.gov/genetics/understanding/traits/intelligence/.

102 Frances E. Anderson, November 3, 2022, https://phys.org/news/2022-11-math-teacher-students-good-lag.html.

103 Daniel Howley, November 2, 2022, https://finance.yahoo.com/news/social-media-as-we-know-it-is-over-185009487.html.

104 Timothy P. Carney, "Americans Are Burned Out Because They Traded Faith and Family for Work," *Washington Examiner*, October 20, 2022, https://www.washingtonexaminer.com/restoring-america/community-family/americans-burned-out-traded-faith-family-for-work.

105 Aaron Bolton, November 10, 2022, https://www.npr.org/sections/health-shots/2022/11/10/1135125625/homelessness-elderly-housing-inflation.

106 Jeffrey Levine, "Aging in Angola Prison," GeriPal, April 16, 2015, https://geripal.org/aging-in-angola-prison/.

107 Wei Lu, "Self-Assembly of Nanostructures," *Springer Link*, accessed November 12, 2022, https://link.springer.com/referenceworkentry/10.1007/978-90-481-9751-4_274.

108 Felix Wursten, November 3, 2022, https://phys.org/news/2022-11-quantum-component-graphene.html.

109 Loren Thompson, "U.S. Shipbuilding Is at Its Lowest Ebb Ever. How Did America Fall so Far?" *Forbes*, July 23, 2021, https://www.forbes.com/sites/lorenthompson/2021/07/23/us-shipbuilding-is-at-its-lowest-ebb-ever-how-did-america-fall-so-far/?sh=1b9d74676c87.

110 *New York Times*, accessed November 12, 2022, https://www.nytimes.com/interactive/2020/06/17/business/economy/how-container-ships-are-built.html.

111 Sandy Smith, *JAXPORT*, July 27, 2020, https://www.jaxport.com/beyond-the-port-shipbuilding-in-jacksonville/.

112 Gabriel Honrada, *Asia Times*, November 16, 2022, https://asiatimes.com/2022/11/chinas-flying-submarine-drones-the-future-of-warfare/.

113 US Debt Clock, accessed November 13, 2022, https://www.usdebtclock.org/.

114 Lauren Bird, "'A Major Problem': The US Is Now a Record $31 Trillion in Debt, Made Worse by Rising Interest Rates—and This Is Who Holds the IOUs," *Yahoo Finance*, November 9, 2022, https://finance.yahoo.com/news/us-national-debt-now-tops-210000112.html.

115 Ben Johnson, "How the US Government Created the Student Loan Crisis," *FEE Stories*, August 29, 2022, https://fee.org/articles/how-the-us-government-created-the-student-loan-crisis/#:~:text=The%20federal%20govern-

ment%20largely%20nationalized,more%20than%20doubled%2C%20fro-m%20%20%24811.

116 Cory Turner, "A Federal Judge Calls Student Loan Relief Unlawful, Deepening Limbo for Borrowers," *NPR*, November 11, 2022, https://www.npr.org/2022/11/10/1135940851/student-debt-relief-biden-blocked-texas-district-court.

117 Gabriel Hays, *Fox News*, November 11, 2022, https://www.foxnews.com/media/demise-bidens-student-loan-handout-rocks-twitter-only-purpose-was-buy-votes.

118 *Wall Street Journal*, November 14, 2022, https://www.wsj.com/articles/joe-bidens-student-loan-write-off-loses-again-missouri-eighth-circuit-court-of-appeals-11668467087?mod=mhp.

119 Haisten Willis, *Washington Examiner*, November 15, 2022, https://www.washingtonexaminer.com/restoring-america/fairness-justice/biden-administration-student-loans-questions.

120 Dan Mangan and Annie Nova, *CNBC*, November 14, 2022, https://www.cnbc.com/2022/11/14/biden-student-loan-debt-relief-plan-appeals-court-rules.html.

121 Annie Nova, *CNBC*, November 17, 2022, https://www.cnbc.com/2022/11/17/biden-administration-to-make-it-easier-for-borrowers-to-discharge-student-debt-in-bankruptcy.html.

122 Ronda Lee, *Yahoo Money*, November 18, 2022, https://money.yahoo.com/student-loans-advocates-cheer-new-guidance-for-debt-bankruptcy-discharges-171537657.html.

123 Bjorn Lomborg, "Net-Zero Climate Policy Offers Much Pain, Little Gain," *New York Post*, October 2, 2022, https://nypost.com/2022/10/02/net-zero-climate-policy-offers-much-pain-little-gain/.

124 Thomas Catenacci, "Energy Experts Sound Alarm on Europe's Energy Crisis as 'Clear and Present Warning' for America," Fox Business, October 4, 2022, https://www.foxbusiness.com/politics/energy-experts-sound-alarm-europes-energy-crisis-clear-present-warning-america.

125 Vivek Ramaswamy, "ESG and the 'Long-Run Interests' Dodge," *Wall Street Journal*, September 29, 2022, https://www.wsj.com/articles/esg-and-the-long-run-interests-dodge-stockholders-apple-disney-chevron-equity-pressure-lgbtqa-company-climate-change-11664459307?mod=mhp.

BIBLIOGRAPHY

Adler, Ben. "Mexico Releases 'Ambitious' Renewable Energy Targets to Fight Climate Change." *Yahoo News*, November 14, 2022. https://news.yahoo.com/mexico-releases-ambitious-renewable-energy-targets-to-fight-climate-change-222911242.html.

Agence France-Presse. "Planet Earth: 8 Billion People and Dwindling Resources." *South China Morning Post*, November 7, 2022. https://www.scmp.com/economy/china-economy/article/3191840/china-population-urbanisation-offers-huge-source-untapped?module=perpetual_scroll_1&pgtype=article&campaign=3191840.

Akhtar, Allana. "A Psychiatric Nurse Says She and Her Colleagues Are Being Pushed to a Breaking Point, and She Quit Her Dream Job Due to Violence." *Insider*, October 7, 2022. https://www.insider.com/psychiatric-nurse-said-injury-violence-on-the-job-worsened-covid-2022-9.

Al Jazeera. "What the Latest IPCC Science Says about Climate Change." November 6, 2022. https://www.aljazeera.com/news/2022/11/6/what-the-latest-ipcc-science-says-about-climate-change.

Al Jazeera. "World on Highway to Climate Hell, UN Chief Guterres Tells COP27." November 7, 2022. https://www.aljazeera.com/news/2022/11/7/world-on-highway-to-climate-hell-un-chief-guterres-tells-cop27.

Anderson, Frances E. "Former Math Teacher Explains Why Some Students Are 'Good' at Math and Others Lag Behind." *Science*

X, November 3, 2022. https://phys.org/news/2022-11-math-teache
r-students-good-lag.html.

Associated Press. "Greenhouse Gases Reach a New Record as Nations
Fall Behind on Climate Pledges." *NPR*, October 26, 2022. https://
www.npr.org/2022/10/26/1131671933/greenhouse-gases-recor
d-climate-pledges-un.

Battista, Mike. "22 Genes Have Been Linked to Intelligence, but DNA
Is Not Your Destiny." *Creyos*, accessed November 11, 2022. https://
creyos.com/resources/articles/22-genes-linked-to-intelligence.

Berwald, Juli. "Coral Restoration Goes Big." *Nautilus*, November 11,
2022. https://nautil.us/coral-restoration-goes-big-246102/.

Betz, Bradford. "COP27: Delegates Weigh 'Climate Compensation' for
Poor Nations Impacted by Global Warming." *Fox News*, November
6, 2022. https://www.foxnews.com/politics/cop27-delegates-weig
h-climate-compensation-poor-nations-impacted-global-warming.

Bird, Lauren. "'A Major Problem': The US Is Now a Record $31 Trillion
in Debt, Made Worse by Rising Interest Rates—and This Is Who
Holds the IOUs." *Yahoo Finance*, November 9, 2022. https://finance.
yahoo.com/news/us-national-debt-now-tops-210000112.html.

Blaufelder, Christopher, Cindy Levy, Peter Mannion, and Dickon Pinner. "A
Blueprint for Scaling Voluntary Carbon Markets to Meet the Climate
Challenge." *McKinsey Sustainability*, January 29, 2021. https://www.
mckinsey.com/capabilities/sustainability/our-insights/a-blueprint-for-sc
aling-voluntary-carbon-markets-to-meet-the-climate-challenge.

Bolton, Aaron. "More Older Americans Become Homeless as Inflation
Rises and Housing Costs Spike." *NPR*, November 10, 2022.
https://www.npr.org/sections/health-shots/2022/11/10/1135125625/
homelessness-elderly-housing-inflation.

Bradstock, Felicity. "The Global Water Crisis Could Crush the
Energy Industry." *Oil Price*, September 23, 2022. https://oilprice.
com/Energy/Energy-General/The-Global-Water-Crisis-Coul
d-Crush-The-Energy-Industry.html.

Budryk, Zack. "UN Climate Summit Releases Draft of Long-Sought 'Loss
and Damage' Agreement." *The Hill*, November 14, 2022. https://

thehill.com/policy/energy-environment/3735171-un-climate-sum mit-releases-draft-of-long-sought-loss-and-damage-agreement/.

Carney, Timothy P. "Americans Are Burned Out Because They Traded Faith and Family for Work." *Washington Examiner*, October 20, 2022. https:// www.washingtonexaminer.com/restoring-america/community-family/ americans-burned-out-traded-faith-family-for-work.

Catenacci, Thomas. "Energy Experts Sound Alarm on Europe's Energy Crisis as 'Clear and Present Warning' for America." *Fox Business*, October 4, 2022. https://www.foxbusiness.com/politics/ energy-experts-sound-alarm-europes-energy-crisis-clear-pre sent-warning-america.

Catenacci, Thomas. "Energy Group Issues Roadmap for House Republicans to Boost US Energy Security." *Fox Business*, November 21, 2022. https://www.foxbusiness.com/politics/energy-group-issue s-roadmap-house-republicans-boost-us-energy-security.

Catenacci, Thomas. "Left-Wing Green Agenda Backed by John Kerry Would Be 'Disaster' for Developing World, Experts Say." *Fox News*, November 15, 2022. https://www.foxnews.com/politics/ left-wing-green-agenda-backed-john-kerry-disaster-developing- world-experts-say.

CDP. "G7 Firms Failing Paris Agreement on 2.7°C Warming Path." September 6, 2022. https://www.cdp.net/en/articles/investor/ g7-firms-failing-paris-agreement.

Chaparro, Luis. "The Sinaloa Cartel Is Controlling Water in Drought- Stricken Mexico." *Vice World News*, September 20, 2022. https:// www.vice.com/en/article/4ax479/mexico-sinaloa-cartel-water.

Clifford, Catherine. "Bill Gates' Climate-Investment Firm Will Put More Money into Adapting to Climate Change." *CNBC*, October 25, 2022. https://www.cnbc.com/2022/10/25/bill-gates-climate-tec h-investing-company-bev-moving-into-adaptation.html.

Climate Action Network International. "Landmark Decision at Cop27 to Set Up Loss and Damage Fund." November 20, 2022. https:// climatenetwork.org/2022/11/20/landmark-decision-at-cop27-t o-set-up-loss-and-damage-fund/.

Colman, Zack, and Karl Mathiesen. "Nations Reach Preliminary Deal on Payments as Climate Talks Grind through Overtime." *Politico*, November 19, 2022. https://www.politico.com/news/2022/11/19/nations-close-to-agreement-on-payments-as-climate-talks-near-end-00069589.

Conceicao, Pedro. "Human Development in an Age of Uncertainty." *Brookings*, November 4, 2022. https://www.brookings.edu/blog/future-development/2022/11/04/human-development-in-an-age-of-uncertainty/.

Copley, Michael. "Investors Have Trillions to Fight Climate Change. Developing Nations Get Little of It." *NPR*, November 9, 2022. https://www.npr.org/2022/11/09/1134865038/investors-have-trillions-to-fight-climate-change-developing-nations-get-little-o.

Copley, Michael. "Low-Income Countries Want More Money for Climate Damage. They're Unlikely to Get It." *NPR*, November 16, 2022. https://www.npr.org/2022/11/16/1136817427/low-income-countries-want-more-money-for-climate-damage-theyre-unlikely-to-get-i.

Coto, Danica. "Search for Minerals Increases Interest in Deep-Sea Mining." *Science & Technology*, November 10, 2022. https://learningenglish.voanews.com/a/search-for-minerals-increases-interest-in-deep-sea-mining/6819939.html.

Cunningham, Doug. "Greenland Ice Sheet Shows Extensive Inland Thinning, Faster Sea Level Rise." *AccuWeather*, November 11, 2022. https://www.accuweather.com/en/climate/report-greenland-ice-sheet-shows-extensive-inland-thinning-faster-sea-level-rise/1277157.

Dalton, Matthew, Stacy Meichtry, and Summer Said. "COP27 Agrees on Loss and Damage Fund for Vulnerable Countries, Officials Say." *Wall Street Journal*, November 19, 2022. https://www.wsj.com/articles/cop27-agrees-on-loss-and-damage-fund-for-vulnerable-countries-officials-say-11668866219?mod=mhp.

Da Silva, Chantal. "World 'Nowhere Near' Hitting Climate Targets, U.N. Warns." *NBC News*, October 26, 2022. https://www.nbcnews.com/news/world/world-emissions-paris-climate-targets-un-report-rcna54044.

Dillard, Carter. "The Paris Agreement Is Failing; We Need a New Approach." *The Hill*, April 23, 2022. https://thehill.com/opinion/energy-environment/3460944-the-paris-agreement-is-failing-we-need-a-new-approach/.

Dinneen, James. "US Megadrought Could Upend Life as We Know It—Just Look to History." *New Scientist*, November 17, 2022. https://www.newscientist.com/article/2347393-us-megadrought-could-upend-life-as-we-know-it-just-look-to-history/.

Dinneen, James. "What Is Causing the Megadroughts in North and South America?" *New Scientist*, October 28, 2022. https://www.newscientist.com/article/2344377-what-is-causing-the-megadroughts-in-north-and-south-america/.

Donovan, Moira. "Greenland's Melting Ice Sheet Brings an Unexpected Flow of Wealth Potential." *Hakai Magazine*, November 3, 2022. https://hakaimagazine.com/features/greenlands-melting-ice-sheet-brings-an-unexpected-flow-of-wealth-potential/.

Economist, The. "Changing Weather Could Put Insurance Firms Out of Business." September 19, 2019. https://www.economist.com/finance-and-economics/2019/09/19/changing-weather-could-put-insurance-firms-out-of-business?utm_medium=cpc.adword.pd&utm_source=google&ppccampaignID=17210591673&ppcadID=&utm_campaign=a.22brand_pmax&utm_content=conversion.direct-response.anonymous&gclid=EAIaIQobChMI7ZCj6b2f-wIVmBXUAR2CJAuQEAMYASAAEgLOvvD_BwE&gclsrc=aw.ds.

Elbein, Saul, and Sharon Udasin. "Equilibrium/Sustainability—A Rainy Future for the Desert Southwest." *The Hill*, November 10, 2022. https://thehill.com/policy/equilibrium-sustainability/3730176-equilibrium-sustainability-a-rainy-future-for-the-desert-southwest/.

Euronews. "Protesters Call for Compensation from Wealthy Nations at COP27." November 12, 2022. https://www.euronews.com/2022/11/12/watch-protesters-call-for-compensation-from-wealthy-nations-at-cop27.

Fischetti, Mark. "U.S. Droughts Will Be the Worst in 1,000 Years." *Scientific American*, February 12, 2015. https://www.scientificamerican.com/article/u-s-droughts-will-be-the-worst-in-1-000-years1/.

Fish Site, The. "Global Aquaculture Deemed to Be 'in Decline.'" November 15, 2022. https://thefishsite.com/articles/global-aquaculture-deemed-to-be-in-decline.

Flavelle, Christopher. "Rising Seas Threaten an American Institution: The 30-Year Mortgage." *New York Times*, June 19, 2020. https://www.nytimes.com/2020/06/19/climate/climate-seas-30-year-mortgage.html.

France 24. "Half World's Birds in Decline, Species Moving 'Ever Faster' to Extinction." September 28, 2022. https://www.france24.com/en/live-news/20220928-half-world-s-birds-in-decline-species-moving-ever-faster-to-extinction.

Frangoul, Anmar. "The Energy Transition Will Fail Unless Industry Fixes Wind Power Issues, Siemens Energy CEO Says." *CNBC*, November 17, 2022. https://www.cnbc.com/2022/11/17/energy-transition-will-fail-unless-wind-power-fixes-problems-ceo.html.

Freilich, Michael. "NASA Study: Rising Sea Level Could Exceed Estimates for U.S. Coasts." *NASA*, November 15, 2022. https://www.nasa.gov/feature/jpl/nasa-study-rising-sea-level-could-exceed-estimates-for-us-coasts.

Freymann, Eyck. "The Ocean Edge." *The Wire China*, November 6, 2022. https://www.thewirechina.com/2022/11/06/china-seabed-mining/.

Gatlin, Allison. "Biotech Stocks Embrace the Neuroscience Renaissance with Biogen, Amylyx at the Helm." *Investor's Business Daily*, November 16, 2022. https://www.investors.com/news/technology/biotech-stocks-embrace-neuroscience-renaissance-with-biogen-amylyx-at-the-helm/.

Geiger, Julianne. "U.S. and EU to Crack Down on Fossil Fuel Sector's Methane Emissions." *Oil Price*, November 9, 2022. https://oilprice.com/Latest-Energy-News/World-News/US-And-EU-To-Crack-Down-On-Fossil-Fuel-Sectors-Methane-Emissions.html.

Haaland, Marie. "Majority of Young American Adults Say Climate Change Influences Their Decision to Have Children." *SWNS*, September 6, 2021. https://swnsdigital.com/us/2020/04/majority-of-young-american-adults-say-climate-change-infl uences-their-decision-to-have-children/.

Hannan, Dan. "Demands for 'Climate Reparations' Are Laughable." *Washington Examiner*, November 21, 2022. https://www.washingtonexaminer.com/opinion/demands-for-climate-reparation s-are-laughable.

Harvey, Chelsea. "Western 'Megadrought' Is the Worst in 1,200 Years." *Scientific American*, February 15, 2022. https://www.scientificamerican.com/article/western-megadrought-is-the-wors t-in-1-200-years/.

Hays, Gabriel. "Demise of Biden's Student Loan Handout Rocks Twitter: 'Its Only Purpose Was to Buy Votes.'" *Fox News*, November 11, 2022. https://www.foxnews.com/media/demise-bidens-student-loa n-handout-rocks-twitter-only-purpose-was-buy-votes.

Henson, Bob. "Climate Change Is Stoking What May Be a Long-Term Megadrought in Western U.S." *The Weather Channel*, April 16, 2020. https://weather.com/news/climate/news/2020-04-16-climate-chang e-stoking-long-term-megadrought-western-us?cm_ven=PS_GGL_ DSA_09162019_1&par=MK_GGL&tpcc=mktg-search-Google- acquisition&gclid=EAIaIQobChMIpbCM3dCR-wIVJilMCh 23SQ4IEAMYASAAEgLR1fD_BwE.

Honore, Marcel. "North Shore Group Confronts Growing Threats of Erosion, Sea Level Rise." *Honolulu Civil Beat*, October 31, 2022. https://www.civilbeat.org/2022/10/north-shore-group-confronts-gr owing-threats-of-erosion-sea-level-rise/.

Honrada, Gabriel. "China's Flying Submarine Drones the Future of Warfare." *Asia Times*, November 16, 2022. https://asiatimes. com/2022/11/chinas-flying-submarine-drones-the-future-of-warfare/.

Howley, Daniel. "Social Media as We Know It Is Over." *Yahoo Finance*, November 2, 2022. https://finance.yahoo.com/news/social-media-a s-we-know-it-is-over-185009487.html.

Huang, Robert, and Matthew Kahn. "Get Ready for the Great American Land Rush." *Business Insider*, November 15, 2022. https://www. businessinsider.com/great-american-land-rush-land-housing-win d-power-solar-panels-2022-11.

Huggins, Xander. "Ripple Effect: As Global Freshwater Basins Dry Up, the Threat to Ecosystems and Communities Grows." *Science X*, November 3, 2022. https://phys.org/news/2022-11-ripple-effec t-global-freshwater-basins.html.

Jacabo, Julia, and Daniel Manzo. "Megadrought out West Expected to Intensify, Expand East: NOAA." *ABC News,* April 12, 2022. https://abcnews.go.com/US/megadrought-west-expecte d-intensify-expand-east-noaa/story?id=84221152.

Johnson, Ben. "How the US Government Created the Student Loan Crisis." *FEE Stories*, August 29, 2022. https://fee.org/articles/how-th e-us-government-created-the-student-loan-crisis/#:~:text=The%20 federal%20government%20largely%20nationalized,more%20 than%20doubled%2C%20from%20%24811.

Kaufman, Leslie, and Will Wade. "The Tiny Insurance Company Standing between Taxpayers and a Costly Coal Industry Bailout." *Yahoo Finance,* November 8, 2022, https://finance.yahoo.com/news/ tiny-insurance-company-standing-between-100013813.html.

Kenton, Will. "Carbon Credits and How They Can Offset Your Carbon Footprint." *Investopedia*, August 19, 2022. https://www. investopedia.com/terms/c/carbon_credit.asp#:~:text=Carbon% 20credits%2C%20also%20known%20as,%2Dand%2Dtrade %22%20program.

Kimani, Alex. "Exxon Mobil Makes First Oil Discovery in Angola in 20 Years." *Oil Price*, November 12, 2022, https://oilprice.com/ Energy/Crude-Oil/Exxon-Mobil-Makes-First-Oil-Discovery-In-Angola-In-20-Years.html.

Kolodny, Lora, and Michael Wayland. "Electric Vehicles Are Less Reliable Because of Newer Technologies, Consumer Reports Finds." *CNBC*, November 15, 2022. https://www.cnbc.com/2022/11/15/ consumer-reports-new-technologies-make-evs-less-reliable.html.

KOMO News. "Washington to Prohibit Commercial Finfish Net Pen Aquaculture from State's Waters." November 18, 2022. https://komonews.com/news/local/fish-farms-washington-state-dnr-department-of-natural-resources-commercial-finfish-net-pen-aquaculture-hillary-franz-commissioner-public-lands-salish-bainbridge-tribe-suquamish.

Kottasova, Ivana. "Not a Single G20 Country Is in Line with the Paris Agreement on Climate, Analysis Shows." *CNN*, September 16, 2021. https://www.cnn.com/2021/09/15/world/climate-pledges-insufficient-cat-intl/index.html.

Lee, Ronda. "Student Loans: Advocates Cheer New Guidance for Debt Bankruptcy Discharges." *Yahoo Money*, November 18, 2022. https://money.yahoo.com/student-loans-advocates-cheer-new-guidance-for-debt-bankruptcy-discharges-171537657.html.

Levine, Jeffrey. "Aging in Angola Prison." GeriPal, April 16, 2015. https://geripal.org/aging-in-angola-prison/.

Lomborg, Bjorn. "Net-Zero Climate Policy Offers Much Pain, Little Gain." *New York Post*, October 2, 2022. https://nypost.com/2022/10/02/net-zero-climate-policy-offers-much-pain-little-gain/.

Loris, Nicolas. "Paris Climate Agreement: Instead of Regulations and Mandates, Embrace Markets." *The Heritage Foundation*, February 25, 2021. https://www.heritage.org/energy-economics/report/paris-climate-agreement-instead-regulations-and-mandates-embrace-markets?gclid=EAIaIQobChMImP6jr96R-wIV0gN9Ch3YgQgPEAMYASAAEgL4IPD_BwE.

Lubben, Alex. "Houston's Solution to Climate Change Is to Force Low-Income People to Move." *Vice News*, October 13, 2022. https://www.vice.com/en/article/k7bp5e/houston-mobile-home-buyout-flood-risks.

Lu, Wei. "Self-Assembly of Nanostructures." *Springer Link*, accessed November 12, 2022. https://link.springer.com/referenceworkentry/10.1007/978-90-481-9751-4_274.

Maher, Kris, and Christine Mai-Duc. "California Sues 3M, DuPont over 'Forever Chemicals.'" *Wall Street Journal*, November 10, 2022. https://

www.wsj.com/articles/california-sues-3m-and-dupont-over-pfas-chemi
cals-11668113297.

Mangan, Dan, and Annie Nova. "Federal Appeals Court Blocks Biden
Student Debt Relief Program Nationwide." *CNBC*, November 14,
2022. https://www.cnbc.com/2022/11/14/biden-student-loan-deb
t-relief-plan-appeals-court-rules.html.

McFall, Caitlin. "Biden Announces $20B to Move Indonesia Away from
Coal." *Fox News*, November 15, 2022. https://www.foxnews.com/
politics/biden-announces-20b-move-indonesia-away-coal.

Medline Plus. "Is Intelligence Determined by Genetics?" Accessed
November 11, 2022. https://medlineplus.gov/genetics/understanding/
traits/intelligence/.

Meredith, Sam. "Historic Deal for Poorer Nations as COP Climate
Summit Agrees to 'Loss and Damage' Fund." *CNBC*, updated
November 21, 2022. https://www.cnbc.com/2022/11/20/cop27-ne
w-global-climate-deal-struck-at-conference-in-egypt.html.

Migiro, Geoffrey. "Which Deserts Are in North America?" *World
Atlas*, October 31, 2018. https://www.worldatlas.com/articles/
which-deserts-are-in-north-america.html.

Milloy, Steve. "A Quiet Refutation of 'Net Zero' Carbon Emissions."
Wall Street Journal, December 28, 2022. https://www.wsj.com/articl
es/a-quiet-refutation-of-net-zero-climate-change-emissions-energy-g
lobal-warming-sec-goals-clean-power-11672262963.

MIT. "Mission 2016: The Future of Strategic Natural Resources."
Accessed November 6, 2022. https://web.mit.edu/12.000/www/
m2016/finalwebsite/solutions/newmines.html.

NASA. "Methane 'Super-Emitters' Mapped by NASA's New Earth
Space Mission." October 25, 20222. https://www.nasa.gov/feature/
jpl/methane-super-emitters-mapped-by-nasa-s-new-earth-space-
mission.

Nature. "COP27: Rich Countries Must Stop Stalling Talks on Climate
Loss and Damage Compensation." November 8, 2022. https://www.
nature.com/articles/d41586-022-03596-6.

New York Times. "How Giant Ships Are Built." Accessed November 12, 2022. https://www.nytimes.com/interactive/2020/06/17/business/economy/how-container-ships-are-built.html.

Nield, David. "Almost Half of Earth's Vital Signs Are Now 'Code Red', Scientists Warn." *Science Alert*, October 29, 2022. https://www.sciencealert.com/almost-half-of-earths-vital-signs-are-now-code-red-scientists-warn.

Nouala, Simplice. "Livestock Is a Form of Climate Justice in the Global South." *Al Jazeera*, November 10, 2022. https://www.aljazeera.com/opinions/2022/11/10/livestock-is-a-form-of-climate-justice-in-the-global-south.

Nova, Annie. "Biden Administration to Make It Easier for Student Loan Borrowers to Discharge Debt in Bankruptcy." *CNBC*, November 17, 2022. https://www.cnbc.com/2022/11/17/biden-administration-to-make-it-easier-for-borrowers-to-discharge-student-debt-in-bankruptcy.html.

Novoselov, Anna. "Megadrought in Southwestern North America Is Region's Driest in At Least 1,200 Years." *UCLA Newsroom*, February 14, 2022. https://newsroom.ucla.edu/releases/megadrought-southwestern-north-america.

Nunez, Emily C. "Study Warns of Climate Change's Looming Devastation of Insect Species." *Maryland Today*, November 7, 2022. https://today.umd.edu/study-warns-of-climate-changes-looming-devastation-of-insect-species.

O'Donnell, Grace. "Net Zero Could Lead to 'the Largest Redeployment of Capital in History.'" *Yahoo Finance*, November 1, 2022. https://finance.yahoo.com/news/net-zero-largest-redeployment-of-capital-in-history-bny-mellon-171509117.html.

Oil Price. "The U.S. Might Need to Increase Electricity Generation by 480%." November 11, 2022. https://oilprice.com/Energy/Energy-General/The-US-Might-Need-To-Increase-Electricity-Generation-By-480.html.

Olick, Diana. "Microsoft, Meta and Others Face Rising Drought Risk to Their Data Centers." *CNBC*, November 15, 2022. https://www.

cnbc.com/2022/11/15/microsoft-meta-others-face-rising-drought-ris
k-to-their-data-centers.html.

Olick, Diana. "Mortgage Market Is Unprepared for Climate Risk, Says Industry Report." *CNBC*, September 23, 2021. https:// www.cnbc.com/2021/09/23/mortgage-market-is-unprepare d-for-climate-risk-says-industry-report.html.

Paraskova, Tsvetana. "UN Launches Satellite System to Track Methane Emissions." *Oil Price*, November 11, 2022. https://oilprice.com/ Latest-Energy-News/World-News/UN-Launches-Satellite-System-T o-Track-Methane-Emissions.html.

Parshley, Lois. "The US Megadrought Won't Just End—It Will Change the Land Forever." *New Scientist*, November 1, 2022. https://www. newscientist.com/article/2344912-the-us-megadrought-wont-ju st-end-it-will-change-the-land-forever/.

Peterdy, Kyle. "Carbon Credits." *Corporate Finance Institute*, August 19, 2022. https://corporatefinanceinstitute.com/resources/esg/carbon-credit/.

Philpot, Brian. "Looming Food Crisis: We Need to Keep Farmland in the Hands of Farmers." *The Hill*, November 1, 2022. https://thehill. com/opinion/finance/3714195-looming-food-crisis-we-need-to-ke ep-farmland-in-the-hands-of-farmers/.

Prengaman, Peter. "Confusion, Finger-Pointing, Opposing Views at Egypt's COP27." *AP News*, November 17, 2022. https://apnews. com/article/g-20-summit-climate-and-environment-d8bd753 0e445c0e7987c69677881a88d.

Pruitt-Young, Sharon. "Young People Are Anxious about Climate Change and Say Governments Are Failing Them." *NPR*, September 4, 2021. https://www.npr.org/2021/09/14/1037023551/climat e-change-children-young-adults-anxious-worried-study.

Pultarova, Tereza. "Sea Levels Might Rise Much Faster Than Thought, Data from Greenland Suggest." *Space.com,* November 9, 2022. https://www.space.com/greenland-ice-melting-satellit e-data-climate-change.

Putzier, Konrad. "The U.S. Is Running Short of Land for Housing." *Wall Street Journal*, September 25, 2022. https://www.wsj.com/articles/the-u-s-is-running-short-of-land-for-housing-11664125841.

Ramaswamy, Vivek. "ESG and the 'Long-Run Interests' Dodge." *Wall Street Journal*, September 29, 2022. https://www.wsj.com/articles/esg-and-the-long-run-interests-dodge-stockholders-apple-disney-chevron-equity-pressure-lgbtqa-company-climate-change-11664459307?mod=mhp.

Reinicke, Carmen. "Starwood's Barry Sternlicht Says What the Fed Is Doing to the Economy Is 'Suicide.'" *CNBC*, November 17, 2022. https://www.cnbc.com/2022/11/17/starwoods-sternlicht-says-what-the-fed-is-doing-to-economy-is-suicide.html.

Rugaber, Christopher. "Fed Official Suggests Substantial Rate Hikes May Be Needed." *ABC News*, November 17, 2022. https://abcnews.go.com/Business/wireStory/fed-official-suggests-substantial-rate-hikes-needed-93479550.

Sackur, Leila. "Should Rich Countries Pay Climate 'Reparations'? Why the Debate Is on the COP27 Agenda." *NBC News*, November 15, 2022. https://www.nbcnews.com/news/world/climate-reparations-cop27-what-it-means-rcna49105.

Sherriff, Lucky. "The Seaweed Superfood Revolution Could End World Hunger—and Save the Planet." *Yahoo Finance*, November 7, 2022. https://finance.yahoo.com/news/seaweed-superfood-revolution-could-end-180000023.html.

Simon, Sarah. "Gen Z Is Increasingly Developing Anxiety about Climate Change." *Very Well Health*, April 19, 2021. https://www.verywellhealth.com/gen-z-climate-change-anxiety-survey-5179490.

SINTEF. "Fjord Ice Can Have a Great Impact on Local Communities." *Science X*, November 9, 2022. https://phys.org/news/2022-11-fjord-ice-great-impact-local.html.

Slav, Irina. "New Englanders Are Fed Up with High Energy Prices." *Oil Price*, November 18, 2022. https://oilprice.com/Energy/Heating-Oil/New-Englanders-Are-Fed-Up-With-High-Energy-Prices.html.

Smith, Matthew. "Guyana's Offshore Drilling Bonanza Is Just Getting Started." *Oil Price*, November 5, 2022. https://oilprice.com/Energy/Crude-Oil/Guyanas-Offshore-Drilling-Bonanza-Is-Just-Getting-Started.html.

Smith, Sandy. "Beyond the Port: Shipbuilding in Jacksonville." *JAXPORT*, July 27, 2020. https://www.jaxport.com/beyond-the-port-shipbuilding-in-jacksonville/.

Sor, Jennifer. "The Fed Will Only Stop Tightening if There's a Recession, and Investors Are Stretching if They're Hoping for a Pivot, Citi's US Investment Strategist Warns." *Markets Insider*, November 15, 2022. https://markets.businessinsider.com/news/stocks/recession-fed-tightening-rate-hike-pivot-pause-inflation-falling-citi-2022-11.

Stanford University. "Dams Could Play a Big Role in Feeding the World More Sustainably, Researchers Find." *Science X,* November 14, 2022. https://phys.org/news/2022-11-play-big-role-world-sustainably.html.

Stockholm Resilience Center. "The Nine Planetary Boundaries." Accessed October 31, 2022. https://www.stockholmresilience.org/research/planetary-boundaries/the-nine-planetary-boundaries.html.

Thompson, Loren. "U.S. Shipbuilding Is at Its Lowest Ebb Ever. How Did America Fall so Far?" *Forbes*, July 23, 2021. https://www.forbes.com/sites/lorenthompson/2021/07/23/us-shipbuilding-is-at-its-lowest-ebb-ever-how-did-america-fall-so-far/?sh=1b9d74676c87.

Tollefson, Jeff. "Carbon Emissions Hit New High: Warning from COP27." *Nature*, November 11, 2022. https://www.nature.com/articles/d41586-022-03657-w.

Trainer, Jocelyn. "The Geopolitics of Deep-Sea Mining and Green Technologies." *United States Institute of Peace*, November 3, 2022. https://www.usip.org/publications/2022/11/geopolitics-deep-sea-mining-and-green-technologies.

Turner, Cory. "A Federal Judge Calls Student Loan Relief Unlawful, Deepening Limbo for Borrowers." *NPR*, November 11, 2022. https://www.npr.org/2022/11/10/1135940851/student-debt-relief-biden-blocked-texas-district-court.

University of California—Santa Cruz. "Scientists Show Transmission of Epigenetic Memory across Multiple Generations." *SciTech Daily*, October 4, 2022. https://scitechdaily.com/scientists-show-transmission-of-epigenetic-memory-across-multiple-generations/.

US Debt Clock, accessed November 13, 2022, https://www.usdebtclock.org/.

Van Dam, Andrew. "People Are Fleeing Puerto Rico, Guam and Every Other U.S. Territory. What Gives?" *Washington Post*, September 23, 2022. https://www.washingtonpost.com/business/2022/09/23/american-territories-population-loss/.

Wackernagel, Mathis. "Humanity Uses 70% More of the Global Commons Than the Earth Can Regenerate." *GEF*, November 14, 2017. https://www.thegef.org/news/humanity-uses-70-more-global-commons-earth-can-regenerate.

Wall Street Journal. "Biden's Student Loan Cancellation Loses Again." November 14, 2022. https://www.wsj.com/articles/joe-bidens-student-loan-write-off-loses-again-missouri-eighth-circuit-court-of-appeals-11668467087?mod=mhp.

Weeks, Olivia. "The 40-Year Robbing of Rural America." *In These Times*, October 3, 2022. https://inthesetimes.com/article/financial-capital-sacrifice-zones-robbing-rural-america.

White, Robyn. "Why Is the Mississippi River Drying Up?" *Newsweek*, November 15, 2022. https://www.newsweek.com/mississippi-river-drying-1759697.

Williams, Trey. "The Jobs That Built America's Middle Class Are Disappearing, Intensifying Its Downfall." *Fortune*, November 9, 2022. https://fortune.com/2022/11/09/american-middle-class-jobs-disappearing/.

Willis, Haisten. "Biden Administration Faces Tough Questions as Student Loan Plan Held Up in Court." *Washington Examiner*, November 15, 2022. https://www.washingtonexaminer.com/restoring-america/fairness-justice/biden-administration-student-loans-questions.

Winslow, Ben. "How Much It Might Cost to Build a Pipeline to Fill the Great Salt Lake." *Fox 13*, October 13, 2022. https://www.fox13now.

com/news/local-news/how-much-it-might-cost-to-build-a-pipeli
ne-to-fill-the-great-salt-lake.

Wursten, Felix. "A New Quantum Component Made from Graphene."
Science X, November 3, 2022. https://phys.org/news/2022-11-quantum-
component-graphene.html.

9 781665 742566